Banking Panics of the Gilded Age

This is the first major study of post–Civil War banking panics in almost a century. The author has constructed for the first time estimates of bank closures and their incidence in each of the five separate banking disturbances. The book takes a novel approach by reconstructing the course of banking panics in the interior, where suspension of cash payment, not bank closures, was the primary effect of banking panics on the average person. The author also revaluates the role of the New York Clearing House in forestalling several panics and explains why it failed to do so in 1893 and 1907, concluding that structural defects of the National Banking Act were not the primary cause of the panics.

Elmus Wicker was a Rhodes Scholar at Queen's College, Oxford. He is currently professor of Economics, Emeritus, at Indiana University. He is the author of *Federal Reserve Monetary Policy, 1917–1933*, *Banking Panics of the Great Depression*, and *Principles of Monetary Economics* (with J. Boughton), as well as articles in *American Economic Review, Journal of Economic History*, and numerous other journals.

T0334611

Banking Panics of the Gilded Age

ELMUS WICKER
Indiana University

CAMBRIDGE
UNIVERSITY PRESS

CAMBRIDGE UNIVERSITY PRESS
Cambridge, New York, Melbourne, Madrid, Cape Town, Singapore, São Paulo

Cambridge University Press
The Edinburgh Building, Cambridge CB2 2RU, UK

Published in the United States of America by Cambridge University Press, New York

www.cambridge.org
Information on this title: www.cambridge.org/9780521770231

First published 2000
This digitally printed first paperback version 2006

A catalogue record for this publication is available from the British Library

Library of Congress Cataloguing in Publication data
Wicker, Elmus.
   Banking panics of the Gilded Age / Elmus Wicker.
      p.   cm.
   Includes bibliographical references.
   ISBN 0-521-77023-8 (hb)
   1. Banks and banking – United States – History.   2. Bank failures
– United States – History.   3. Financial crises – United States –
History.   I. Title.
HG2477.W53   2000
332.1′0973 – dc21   99-087487

ISBN-13 978-0-521-77023-1 hardback
ISBN-10 0-521-77023-8 hardback

ISBN-13 978-0-521-02547-8 paperback
ISBN-10 0-521-02547-8 paperback

To Roger and Vanessa

Beautiful Credit. The Foundation of modern Society. Who shall say that this is not the golden age of natural trust, of unlimited reliance upon human promises?

– Mark Twain and Charles Dudley Warner,
The Gilded Age, p. 243

Contents

Preface

Mark Twain (1873) coined the phrase "The Gilded Age" to dramatize the foibles and excesses of the post–Civil War generation. His portrait of Colonel Sellers was an archetype for a generation of dreamers, panglossian optimists, and tireless promoters who pinned their hopes on gaining a speedy fortune by exploiting the opportunities of an ever expanding frontier.

Twain had in mind particularly the excesses of the Grant administration, and historians were slow to perceive a wider application. The Gilded Age is now one label for the era between the Civil War and the fin de siècle, though the terminal date has remained fuzzy. I have taken the liberty to extend it even further to include the 1907 panic because of the special role financiers, especially J. P. Morgan and his banking associates, played in its containment and the adamant refusal of the New York Clearing House bankers to subordinate their individual self-interest to the public good.

Frenzied railroad building ahead of demand represented speculative excess and was an important contributing cause of the panic of 1873. However, the 1893 panic cannot so easily be identified with speculation and speculative excesses on the part of individual bankers. Nevertheless, the banking panics of the post–Civil War era were not events separate and distinct from the forces shaping the behavior of society and the economy as a whole. And the Gilded Age captures perhaps as well as any other label what some of its characteristic features were.

Banking panics were a relatively infrequent feature of American banking experience during the Gilded Age. These episodes of banking instability were accompanied by money market stringency, a stock market collapse, loan and deposit contraction, runs on banks, bank failures, the issue of clearing house certificates, and in the case of the three major banking panics the partial suspension of cash payments. But the partial suspension of cash payment was not dictated by the depletion of the reserves of the New York Clearing House (NYCH) banks, except perhaps in 1873. However, the identifying characteristic of all major banking panics was the general loss of depositor confidence manifest by a sudden and unanticipated switch from deposits to currency. The real effects, if any, as distinct from the purely financial effects, have been more difficult to quantify.

Banking panics belong to the class of financial disturbances which includes panics in the stock market, the foreign exchange market, and the acceleration of commercial bankruptcies. Banking panics are only one type of financial crisis and certainly not the most frequent. Kemmerer (U.S. National Monetary Commission, 1911, pp. 222–23) identified six major panics and fifteen minor panics between 1890 and 1908. Besides the three major panics recognized by Sprague (1873, 1893, 1907) he added three more (1899, 1901, 1903). There was neither a banking panic in any of the former three nor was there a banking panic in any of his fifteen minor panics. What Kemmerer called panics in these eighteen episodes was a period of money market stringency coupled with a sharp break in stock prices; there is no evidence of a general loss of depositor confidence leading to widespread bank runs and bank failures.

Calomiris and Gorton (1991, p. 132) labeled 1896 as a "quasi" panic and 1914 as a full-scale panic. But there was no banking panic in either year. Banking difficulties in 1896 were confined entirely to Chicago and Minneapolis–St. Paul with no further repercussions in the country as a whole. Nor was there a banking panic in 1914. Bank failures were forestalled by the issue of clearing house certificates and Aldrich-Vreeland notes. The first was a purely local banking panic, and the second a financial panic confined mainly to the stock market and to a disruption of the foreign exchanges. Their definition of a banking panic was purely empirical, that is, an event that coincided with collective action by the New York Clearing House without reference to any criterion about their costs or consequences.

What the national banking era experience tells us is that there were no more than three major banking panics between 1873 and 1907 and two incipient banking panics in 1884 and 1890. Twelve years elapsed between the panic of 1861 and the panic of 1873, twenty years between the panics of 1873 and 1893, and fourteen years between 1893 and 1907: three banking panics in almost half a century! And in only one of the three, 1893, did the number of bank suspensions match those of the Great Depression. The suspension of cash payment, not ubiquitous bank runs and bank failures, was how the average person experienced the banking panics of 1873 and 1907.

The banking panics of the national banking era were only one phase of American banking panic experience and by no means the most serious. We can isolate three distinct phases characterized by the type of regulatory framework in place: pre–Civil War, the National Banking Era, and the Federal Reserve System era. In the pre–Civil War regime federal regulation was absent with panics in 1819, 1837, 1857, 1860, and 1861. In the second phase, the National Banking Era, banking disturbances occurred in 1873, 1884, 1890, 1893, and 1907. The third phase included the five banking panics of the Great Depression which I examined in a previous study (1996). We concentrate our attention on the second phase which encompasses the period between the passage of the National Banking Act in 1863 and the establishment of the Federal Reserve System. The chronological boundaries conveniently follow the tradition initiated by Sprague (1910).

The consensus among financial historians has been that certain structural weaknesses of the National Banking Act increased the vulnerability of the U.S. banking system to panics, three of which have received the most attention: (1) the inelasticity of the national bank note currency, (2) the pyramiding of reserves in New York, and (3) the fixed and invariant reserve requirements. The currency stock was composed of specie, a fixed quantity of greenbacks issued to finance the Civil War, national bank notes, and, before 1866 when they were taxed out of existence, state bank notes. The incentive to issue national bank notes depended on the price of government bonds used as collateral. And bond prices did not always behave in a manner conducive to new note issue. The structure of reserve requirements was conducive to the concentration of reserves among the NYCH banks. The weight of this consideration has been diminished substantially by Myers (1931), who showed that had the National Banking Act of 1864 been in effect in December 1860 the reserves of the New York banks would have closely approximated the actual bankers' balances held in that year. The inflexibility of reserve requirements immobilized a portion of the banking reserve, thereby constraining its use in emergencies.

It is not at all clear that the National Banking Act made the banking system more prone to panics. At a more fundamental level legislation prohibiting statewide branching laws was a necessary but not a sufficient condition for the existence of banking panics (Calomiris, 1993). We intend to show that the problem was not solely with the structure of the national banking system but institutional failure on the part of the NYCH; it had the power, instruments, and access to knowledge to have prevented banking panics. It could not agree after 1873 on an agenda that was incentive-compatible. Purely voluntary collective action apparently was not a viable option for banking reform.

Sprague's classic study – *A History of Crises Under the National Banking System* – appeared almost ninety years ago in response to an invitation of the National Monetary Commission. It has served its purpose so well as the principal source of our knowledge of what happened during this era that no work of comparable scale has replaced it. There are, however, ample reasons for undertaking a new study of the banking panics of the national banking era. There are the serious gaps in Sprague's earlier analysis that we can now attempt to remedy. Sprague, and everyone else for that matter, did not know the number or the incidence of bank suspensions in each of the five banking disturbances in either New York or the interior. He described carefully what happened in the New York money market, but he paid little or no attention to bank runs and bank failures outside New York, a task we are fully prepared to remedy. Furthermore, at the time Sprague wrote, documents and records illuminating more clearly what happened in 1907 were not available. He was certainly aware of the role J. P. Morgan played in the 1907 panic from newspaper accounts. We now have a better understanding of that role as revealed by Morgan's biographers and the biographies of his principal lieutenants, and the testimony given in the Stanley Hearings (U.S. House of Representatives, 1911) where we find eyewitness accounts of the Morgan initiatives to provide financial support to the troubled trust companies, the Stock Exchange, and the New York municipal authority. A reassessment of those initiatives faults Morgan for allowing the Knickerbocker Trust Company to succumb and for his reliance on the device of the "money pool" as a less efficient instrument than the prompt issue of clearing house certificates by the New York Clearing House. The NYCH was equally at fault for having relinquished leadership in the crisis to Morgan, whose efforts were successful though second-best. The role of the NYCH can better be discerned through its official records and documents not available to Sprague at the time.

Sprague was the first to have shown that the NYCH had access to the knowledge, instruments, and power to have prevented banking panics. It did so in 1860 and 1861. The power to equalize or pool the reserves of the NYCH banks effectively in his opinion turned the Clearing House into a central bank by mobilizing and reallocating the reserves of the central money market banks. The problem of the money center banks was not, except perhaps in 1873, an inadequate stock of total reserves; it was their distribution among the six or seven New York City banks holding the bulk of the bankers' balances.

Along the way we have also found some minor revisions were necessary in conventional interpretations of the banking panic experience. For example, banking unrest in 1884 and 1890 is perhaps better described as *incipient* rather than full banking panics since there was no general loss of depositor confidence in either New York or the interior, and the NYCH acted with dispatch to forestall a banking panic. It is a success story that has gone largely unheralded. Sprague's doubts about how to classify the 1890 banking disturbance are revealed by his selection of a chapter heading: "Financial Stringency in 1890." Although he did label the 1884 disturbance a panic, it was unaccompanied by the adjective banking. He certainly underplayed its purely banking aspects.

My interest in the banking panics of the national banking era arose quite naturally from my previous study of the banking panics of the Great Depression. The question obviously posed itself: Was there a difference between banking panics in the two contiguous periods? But it immediately became apparent that our knowledge of what happened in the former period was much less than in the latter, especially with respect to the number and incidence of bank suspensions and the course of the banking panics in the interior, gaps that would require remedying if at all possible. Moreover, increasing scholarly attention was being paid to two questions: What role did the clearing house play, if any, in promoting banking stability? and Can we construct a theoretical model of banking panics to explain their existence? Seeking answers to these questions rekindled interest in the historical banking panic evidence.

There is a burgeoning literature on the role clearing houses might have played in preventing banking panics. Much of that literature, however, addresses the purely theoretical question: Can private market arrangements insure banking stability in the absence of a central bank? Timberlake (1993), for example, has asked why the clearing house system was rejected in favor of a government central bank (the Federal Reserve) when the clearing house system had proven so effective. Gorton and Mullineaux (1987) and Goodhart (1988) have given conflicting accounts of the efficacy of a purely voluntary association of banks as a safeguard against banking panics. According to the former the clearing house system would not work without regulations. But in the absence of government interference, a system of "endogenous" regulations would have to be put in place to insure bank cooperation, such as reserve requirements, bank surveillance, and penalties for noncompliance. Admittedly, these arrangements might not be completely successful, but they would mitigate the panic's worst effects.

Goodhart is not so sanguine. He does not believe that a really satisfactory solution could be found through purely voluntary action. Conflicting interests among competing banks would deter or postpone any effective response. Self-interest (profit) considerations could not always be reconciled with group interests as a whole. He concluded that a nonprofit maximizing body was required in the form of a central bank. Timberlake, Gorton and Mullineaux, and Goodhart alike did not produce any detailed historical evidence about specific panics to support or reject their claims. Our evidence from the post–Civil War panics may throw some light on these issues.

Banking panics were regarded until quite recently as a manifestation of irrational or inscrutable behavior. The word "panic" itself means, according to the New Shorter Oxford English dictionary: "An excessive and increasing feeling of alarm or fear leading to extravagant or foolish behavior, such as that which may suddenly spread through crowds of people." Depositor runs on an individual bank spread to other banks by a process analogous to the spread of contagious diseases. And bank run contagion was considered for quite some time as the discriminating characteristic of historical banking panics. That view has now come to be questioned by Dowd (1996), who has claimed that bank run contagion has been vastly exaggerated, and that bank runs and bank failures were rare events not only in the United States but in many other countries as well. But the evidence upon which to base such judgment has been largely lacking. Only a detailed narrative of individual banking panics can contribute to resolving the problem.

In the contemporary finance literature banking panics have increasingly come to be treated as a rational response to asymmetric information, for example, Jacklin and Bhattacharya (1988) and Calomiris and Gorton (1991). Depositors do not have access to the same information as do the banks on the quality of the bank's loan portfolio. In response to news that a particular bank had suffered a severe loan loss or serious managerial malfeasance (asset shocks) depositors would withdraw their deposits from the offending bank and its close affiliates. With an asset shock that is more general, depositors may not be able to distinguish between sound and unsound banks and a contagious bank run ensues. The problem is to identify the asset shock or shocks and their effects, if any, on particular troubled banks.

There is an alternative approach attributable to Diamond and Dybvig (1983), who model banking panics as a response to liquidity shocks due to a maturity mismatch between bank assets and bank liabilities. These liquidity shocks depend solely on extraneous uncertainty (sunspots). The problem with the Diamond and Dybvig approach is to find an empirical counterpart to the alleged liquidity shock with which to distinguish it from an asset shock. Calomiris and Gorton (1991) attempt unsuccessfully to identify the liquidity shock with unexpectedly large demands for currency in the countryside due to seasonal demands during the crop moving season. But as we shall attempt to show, the most serious of the post–Civil War panics (1893) did not occur during the crop moving season!

Almost all students of banking panics have noted the similarity in the timing of banking panics with seasonal crop movement considerations. There were two periods of seasonal demands for funds, in May at crop-planting time and September to November when the crops were harvested and shipped to the East Coast. The stronger of the two was autumnal movement of the crops which was frequently accompanied by money market stringency. The conditions for a banking panic were greatest when seasonal money market stringency was combined with a shock to the banking sector. Autumn banking disturbances occurred in September 1873, November 1890, and October 1907. Two were not in the autumn: 1884 (May) and 1893 (June–August). The most severe banking panic in terms of bank suspensions and geographical incidence was the 1893 panic when crop movement considerations were absent. Of the three major banking panics, two occurred in the fall (1873 and 1907) and one during the summer (1893). Of the two incipient panics one had its origin in May (1884) and the other in November (1890).

I am grateful to those who have read an individual chapter or chapters and made suggestions for improvements. These include Charles Calomiris, William Hutchinson, William Roberds, Hugh Rockoff, Anna Schwartz, and Ellis Tallman.

I also thank the officials of the New York Clearing House who granted my request to examine the minutes of the Clearing House Association as well as the Executive and Loan Committees. Special thanks are reserved for Mirjana Orovic, who as custodian of the archives did everything possible to make my visit comfortable as well as rewarding.

The staff of the Interlibrary Loan Department of the Indiana University Libraries worked indefatigably to keep me supplied with microfilm copies of countless newspapers from all parts of the country over a four-year period.

Bloomington, Indiana   E. W.
November 1999

1 The Bank Panic Experience: An Overview

Before we undertake a comprehensive narrative and analysis of the three major and two incipient banking panics of the national banking era, it may prove useful to provide a broad overview of the bank panic experience. We take bank panic experience to mean not only what happened during banking panics but also the public's perception of those events, especially outside New York where bank runs and bank failures were neither very large nor widely diffused, except in 1893.

Specific banking panics differed as to their origins, duration, the number and incidence of bank runs and bank failures, the response of the New York Clearing House (NYCH), and their real effects. Each had its own signature, as it were, differentiating it from the others. With due respect to those differences, we can still attempt to construct a general profile of what happened both in New York and the interior. Banking panics had their origins in the New York money market with the sole exception being the panic of 1893. Our knowledge of what happened in New York is on firmer ground than our knowledge of what happened outside New York. We also have a fairly clear idea about the course of each of the banking panics in the city of Chicago. But the banking panic experience in the other major cities has been unchronicled, partly from a lack of scholarly interest, and partly from the inconvenience of accessing multiple local newspaper sources. The information deficit is formidable for the interior.

In New York, the banking panic began with an unexpected financial shock: the collapse of a brokerage or merchant banking house or houses and/or the failure of a state or national bank or trust company, the immediate effect being a loss of depositor confidence manifest by bank runs that were usually bank-specific and sometimes extending to all savings banks. The number of bank runs and suspensions excluding brokerage firms was always relatively small; the savings banks responded by restricting deposit withdrawals. A stock exchange panic

1

accompanied the initial shock with sharp spikes in the call money rate and a curtailment of credit availability. The NYCH responded by authorizing the issue of loan certificates to conserve the cash of the member banks and to deter loan contraction. That was followed in the three major banking panics by a restriction of cash payment, which spread quickly to the interior. A currency premium emerged. Gold imports were engaged with a two- to three-week lag, and the Secretary of the Treasury tendered assistance by placing funds in select New York banks when, that is, surplus revenues permitted. Cash payment resumed only after the reserve deficit of the NYCH banks had disappeared. The real effects of the banking panics are more difficult to discern. Estimates of annual gross national product begin in 1869 and unemployment percentages in 1890.

With the sole exception of 1893, banking panics had their origin in the central money market and from there spread to the interior. There were at least four channels of transmission: (1) The banking disturbance in New York unsettled the confidence of the interior banks, especially the country banks, who reacted by withdrawing their balances and by contracting loans and deposits; (2) if the troubled banks in New York had affiliates in other cities the closure of the affiliates was a major channel of transmission (for example, the failure of J. Cooke and Co., a merchant bank in New York, led to the suspension of Cooke affiliates in Philadelphia and Washington, D.C., in 1873); (3) the collapse of a large New York bank with a correspondent network diffused the panic geographically; and (4) the suspension of cash payment in New York led to suspension in the rest of the country.

The evidence from my new bank failure estimates supports the conclusion that bank closures in the interior, except in 1893, were generally few in number, region-specific, and too localized geographically to have exerted economy-wide effects. Sprague (1910) acknowledged that bank failures per se were not a reliable indicator of the banking panic experience outside New York. It was the suspension of cash payments and not bank runs nor bank failures through which the public in the rest of the country experienced the effects of banking panics. The suspension of cash payment restricted partially depositor access to their funds, created problems for businesses attempting to meet payrolls, and generated a currency premium. In a word, the suspension of cash payment traumatized the public. These effects were felt with varying degrees of intensity throughout the country. However, the 1893 panic was the exception. The number of bank closures was large (more than 500), and bank runs were serious though highly concentrated in a small number of cities. Savings banks were especially hard hit. Depositors were indifferent between solvent and insolvent banks, for more than 40 percent of all closed banks reopened within a few months.

Bank Suspension Estimates

Bank runs and bank suspensions are at least two distinctive character-istics of banking panics. Yet we know very little about the incidence of bank runs especially outside New York, nor do we know the total number of bank suspensions. A bank suspension refers to a bank closing that may be temporary or permanent. At the time of closing that information is not available. A bank failure is permanent closure, usually termed receivership, which may be a lengthy legal proceeding. There are reliable data on bank closures and receiverships for all national banks. *Brad-street's*, a contemporary journal of trade and finance published monthly, provided estimates of all bank failures for 1884 and 1893, but these data to my knowledge have never been used. I constructed estimates for the banking disturbances of 1873, 1890, and 1907. I cannot claim that the esti-mates are complete in the sense of my having identified each and every bank suspension in the United States. But I have made a serious effort to identify bank failures that were reported in major and minor news-papers as well as the leading financial journals of the day. Reports of state commissioners of banking are not available for all states, and hence cannot provide a comprehensive basis for estimating the number of sus-pensions of state banks, savings banks, and trust companies. Neverthe-less, some of the reports have been quite helpful in checking my own estimates.

We classify banks by type: national, state, savings, private, and trust companies. We follow *Bradstreet's* definition of the private bank category:

This class is made up largely of members of various speculative exchanges, to which their operations are almost exclusively confined. They are called "brokers" and banks. They accept customer accounts and receive deposits with the full knowledge and understanding of the depositors that their business is based on their success as speculators therewith, and pay amounts due on checks, either in cash or their own checks on other banks as is convenient. Their business is purely speculative.

These deposits at brokers were in effect variable priced deposits, the value of which fluctuated with fluctuations in the price of the assets held by the brokers; private banks were not commercial banks.

Tables 1.1 to 1.3 show the total number of bank failures by type of bank organization for the United States (Table 1.1 and separately for New York City (Table 1.2)) and by location, that is, New York City and

Table 1.1. *Bank suspensions by type of bank organization during the banking panics: 1873–1907*

	Type of bank organization						
	National	State	Savings	Private	Trust	Unclassified	Total
1873 (September)	16	11	7	59	4	4	101
1884 (May)	5	7	4	26			42
1890 (November)	1	3	1	13			18
1893 (May–August)	142	149	41	157	14		503
1907 (October–December)	11	33	4	10	15		73

Source: *Bradstreet's* for 1884 and 1893. Author's estimates for 1873, 1890, and 1907.

the interior (Table 1.3). Tables 1.1 and 1.2 reveal the importance of private bank suspensions (brokerage houses) in 1873, 1884, and 1890; they constituted about 60 percent of the total in the earlier two episodes and were probably much higher in 1890 had we better estimates of bank failures in the interior in that year. Panic in the stock market accounts for the high incidence of suspensions among brokerage firms. It is clear from Table 1.2 that private bank suspensions in New York City constituted almost all of the bank failures in 1873, 1884, and 1890. In 1893, bank closures were about equally divided among national, state, and private banks, the reason being that the 1893 panic originated in the interior with minimal suspensions in New York.

The resilience of the New York banks during periods of banking unrest is readily apparent. If we exclude brokerage houses, the number of bank suspensions in New York City was so small that we are obliged to ask: How could so much alleged financial havoc have been attended by such a small bank failure residue?

Table 1.3 reveals a vast disparity in the bank failure experience among the two incipient and three major banking panics, a minimum of 18 in 1890 to a maximum of 503 in 1893. The paucity of bank failures is even

Table 1.2. *Bank suspensions in New York City by type of bank organization during the banking panics 1873–1907*

	Type of bank organization					
	National	State	Savings	Private	Trust	Total
1873 (September)		1		34	2	37
1884 (May)	1	3	1	10		15
1890 (November)		1		9		10
1893 (May–August)		2			1	3
1907 (October–December)	6	1		2	4	13

Source: *Bradstreet's* for 1884 and 1893. Author's estimates for 1873, 1890, and 1907.

Table 1.3. *Bank suspensions in New York City and the interior during the banking panics 1873–1907*

	New York City	Interior	Total
1873 (September)	37	64	101
1884 (May)	15	27	42
1890 (November)	10	8	18
1893 (May–August)	3	500	503
1907 (October–December)	13	60	73

Source: From data in Tables 1.1 and 1.2.

Table 1.4. *Percentage of total bank suspensions to the total number of banks in each of the banking panics of the national banking era and the Great Depression*

National Banking Era		Great Depression	
Panic	*Percent*	*Panic*	*Percent*
1873*	N.A.	1930	0.034
1884	0.006	1931 I	0.0295
1890	0.0015	II	0.0427
1893	0.042		
1907	0.0026		

*The percentage of state and national bank suspensions of total number of state and national banks was 0.01648 in 1873. I have not uncovered estimates of the total number of unincorporated banks in 1873.

more apparent if we exclude brokerage houses: 16 failures in 1884 and four in 1890! That is one of the reasons, though not the only one, why we classify these two periods of banking unrest as incipient and not full-scale banking panics. The 1893 panic stands entirely alone among the panics of the national banking era but resembles closely those of the Great Depression. Although the 1873 and 1907 are alike in numbers, the failure of brokerage houses was predominant in 1873 and relatively minor in 1907.

What does the bank suspension evidence tell us about the relative severity of the panics of the national banking era? Our data are much more reliable for the banking panics of the Great Depression. One measure of banking panic severity is the percentage of total bank suspensions relative to the total number of banks prior to the banking panic. These percentages are set out in Table 1.4 for each of the banking panics except 1873. I have not been able to obtain estimates for the total number of unincorporated banks in that year. The table also shows the percentages for three of the banking panics of the Great Depression. It is quite clear that the panics of the national banking era were less severe, the single exception being 1893. In 1884, 1890, and 1907, the ratio fell considerably short of 1 percent, whereas in the panics of the Great Depression the ratio was between 3 and 4 percent. The 1893 panic had the same degree of seriousness as the banking panic following Britain's abandonment of the gold standard in September 1931. The absolute disparity in the number of closures between the two eras was quite large. The average number of suspensions was fifty in the earlier era and over 700 in the latter.

The evidence on the number of bank suspensions in the interior removes an important gap in our knowledge of banking panics between the Civil War and World War I. Except in 1893, there was no general loss of depositor confidence of a magnitude that resulted in nationwide bank suspensions. We cannot but be surprised at the smallness of their numbers after adjusting for the closing of brokerage houses. It is clear that unlike the banking panics of the Great Depression the number of bank suspensions alone had no significant effect on the stock of money. Deposits of failed banks were relatively small compared with those of the Great Depression, a conjecture based solely on the fewness of bank closures because we still do not have estimates of deposits in failed banks in the interior.

No data have ever been compiled on the number of bank runs. However, the Comptroller of the Currency's office (1920, pp. 56–73) listed the reasons why national banks failed during panics. Only one national bank failure was attributable to a bank run. But the data refer only to those banks that went into receivership, not to those that had suspended temporarily and later reopened. We approach the problem in a different way. We attempt a complete description of what happened during banking panics contained in our detailed narrative of each panic. Bank runs were indeed an important characteristic of banking panics, but as we might suspect they were far more general during the 1893 crisis.

Suspension of Cash Payment

The bank failure evidence has revealed that bank suspensions in both New York and the interior were neither very large nor widely diffused geographically, if we exclude brokerage houses, with the single exception of the panic of 1893. For the most part the general public had little or no direct experience of bank runs and bank failures. And what they knew, they learned from local newspaper sources. How then did persons in the interior experience a banking panic? Sprague (1910, p. 196) suggested that the "dearth of money" was the panics' most striking feature and the way it "came home directly to the mass of the people." He was referring to the suspension of cash payment in the three major banking panics: 1873, 1893, and 1907. Suspension of cash payment in New York followed by suspension in the interior was the defining characteristic of the panic experience as far as most Americans were concerned.

Suspension of cash payment was a measure taken usually by a group of urban banks acting through a local clearing house association. It could be either complete or partial. If complete, there could be no cash payment for whatever reason. Or it could be partial, as indeed it nearly always was, with restrictions placed on the amount of cash withdrawals. For individuals, checks would be paid but only up to a specific amount, usually $50 or $100. Banks in the interior might also shut off all remittances to New York banks and sharply curtail payments to other banks including correspondents. New York banks might also restrict payments to individual depositors while still making discretionary payments to interior banks, as it had done in 1873. Whatever the arrangements, they were neither uniform in geographical coverage nor consistent in application across the different banking panics. Initiative for the suspension of cash payment came from the NYCH. Action by the NYCH always led to suspension in at least some parts of the country. As we see below, it is not at all clear that suspension of cash payment was the only viable alternative available to the NYCH, nor that it was the most preferred.

The dates of the onset of each panic, the issue of loan certificates, the suspension of cash payment, and the resumption of cash payment are set out in Table 1.5. The time elapsing between the onset of the panic and the issue of loan certificates in 1907 was five days. By conventional panic dates for 1893, six weeks lapsed. By my own dating, it was a little more than two weeks. Similarly the time span was short between the decision of the NYCH to issue loan certificates and to suspend cash payments: four days in 1873, six weeks in 1893, and simultaneously in 1907. The disparity of the 1893 timing reflects the fact that its origin was in the interior rather than in New York, and initially there was less pressure on the New York banks. Sprague considered it an egregious error that the NYCH delayed for five days the issue of loan certificates in 1907 after the collapse of the Knickerbocker Trust and the onset of the runs on two of the largest trust companies. Suspension, he thought, was a discredible step not dictated by the level of bank reserves. Moreover, he thought it admirable that the NYCH continued to pay out cash freely to interior banks in 1873 even after cash payment had been suspended, a situation as we see below that was possible only as a result of the equalization of the reserves of the member banks.

Another of the effects of suspension of cash payment, especially during the 1907 panic, was to create the incentive to issue cash substitutes. The prohibitive costs of making payment with checkable deposits and the difficulties of obtaining cash were preconditions for the emergence of cash substitutes. The emergency currency took the form of small denominational clearing house certificates and paychecks (scrip) issued by manufacturers. Andrew (1908a, p. 458) estimated that these cash

Table 1.5. *Dates of the onset of the issue of Clearing House loan certificates and the suspension of cash payments of each panic 1873–1907*

	Panic onset	Dates of the issue of Clearing House loan certificates	Suspension of cash payments	Resumption of cash payments
1873	September 18 (Jay Cooke)	September 20	September 24	November 1
1884	May 6 (Grant & Ward)	May 14		
1890	November 10	November 11		
1893	May 1 (Nat'l. Cordage)	June 15	August 3	September 2
1907	October 21 (Knickerbocker Trust)	October 26	October 26	January 1

substitutes amounted to $336 million at a minimum for a relatively small sample of banks; many banks in small towns did not report.

The more lasting effects of the banking panics are difficult to track, especially their effects on output and employment. Conceivably, banking panics could trigger declines in output or accentuate or prolong a downswing. However, the preponderance of the timing evidence as given by the National Bureau of Economic Research reference cycle dates (Table 1.6) supports the hypothesis that banking panics did not initiate a downturn in output except perhaps in 1873. Did they aggravate the downswing? The absence of the relevant data makes it highly unlikely that an empirical test could be devised that could separate the effects of a banking panic superimposed on a preexisting downturn.

Romer (1989) and Balke and Gordon (1989) have provided annual real gross national product (GNP) estimates for the years 1869 through 1929 and removed some of our ignorance about what happened to output during the panic and post-panic years. Quarterly estimates would have been preferable, but they are not available. Chart 1 traces the behavior of the Romer and Balke-Gordon estimates. Data are from Tables 2.7, 3.7, and 5.11. What is striking about these estimates is their continuous increase with few exceptions during the forty-five-year

Table 1.6. *National Bureau of Economic Research dating of cyclical peaks and peak banking panic month 1873–1907*

Panics	Cyclical turning point	Peak panic month
1873	October 1873	September 1873
1884	March 1882	May 1884
1890	July 1890	November 1890
1893	January 1893	May 1893
1907	May 1907	October 1907

Source: For cyclical turning points, see Maisel, 1982, p. 290. My dating of peak panic months.

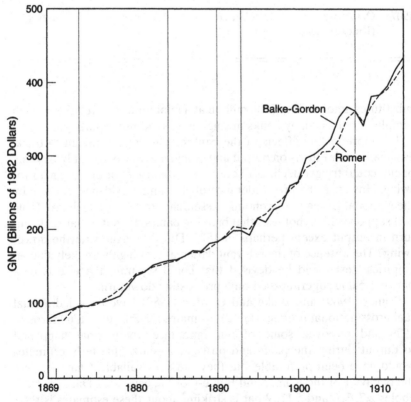

Chart 1. Real GNP estimates: Balke-Gordon and Romer (1869–1913).

period. The Romer estimates show absolute declines in only four years: 1888, a non-panic year; 1893–94; and 1908. There were no declines during the three banking disturbances in 1873, 1884, and 1890. According to the Balke-Gordon estimates, there were declines in six years, three panic or post-panic years: 1874, 1893–94, and 1907, and two non-panic years: 1888 and 1896. There is no disagreement about the behavior of real output during 1893 and 1907 or about the absence of real output effects in 1884 and 1890. Balke and Gordon show more serious output effects in 1893–94 and 1907 than do the Romer estimates: 2.9 percent in 1893–94 and 6.9 percent in 1907.

There were no continuous annual unemployment estimates for the 1869–1913 period. Romer (1986) revised the Lebergott unemployment percentage estimates for the period 1890–1913. They show an 8 percent unemployment rate in 1893 and 12 percent in 1894, whereas in 1907 it was only 6.7 percent. The output and unemployment estimates reveal an interesting conundrum, that is, why were high unemployment percentages associated with relatively mild decreases in real GNP in 1893, whereas smaller increases in the unemployment percentage was associated with much larger declines in real GNP in 1907?

Sprague identified four proximate effects of the suspension of cash payment: (1) payroll difficulties, (2) dislocation of the domestic exchanges, (3) an increase in hoarding, and (4) the emergence of a currency premium. The immediate impact of the suspension of cash payment was partial disruption of the payments mechanism. Whatever disrupts the payments process causes an increase in real transactions costs and may lead to a decline in economic activity. If business firms experience difficulty in obtaining currency to meet payrolls, their response may be temporary factory closings, layoffs, or the creation of innovative substitutes for currency. The domestic exchanges were also disrupted because the banks were reluctant to make remittances. Failure to remit on time encouraged firms to demand cash payment, thereby reducing real transactions.

Restrictions on deposit withdrawals inevitably increased the currency holdings of individuals and business firms who simply stopped paying currency into the banks. Cash payment replaced payment by check, though not completely. The existence of a currency premium was an added inducement not to deposit funds in banks. Currency brokers sought to tempt holders of cash to part with it.

Unfortunately, there are no official nor unofficial estimates of currency in circulation monthly before 1907. Friedman and Schwartz (1963) provide seasonally adjusted annual estimates centered on the month of June for vault cash and currency held by the public between 1887 and

1906. Their monthly estimates begin in May 1907. Deposit-reserve and deposit-currency ratios are estimated by month as well. The data with which to measure the extent of hoarding simply do not exist. The data for 1907 panic reveal that between September and December 1907 the public's currency holdings were greater than either the 1930 or October 1931 banking panics, although the number of bank closings was five times greater in the latter period. What impressed contemporary observers like Sprague (1910) and Andrew (1908b) was the increased hoarding by the country banks. Friedman and Schwartz (1963, p. 160) more recently concluded: "loss of confidence was displayed less by the public than the country banks." The panic-like response of the country banks is a dimension to which insufficient attention has been paid.

The Response of the New York Clearing House

The NYCH, originally organized to perform the purely technical function of clearing and collecting of checks among its members, came to recognize early on limited responsibilities for maintaining banking stability in the New York money market. The money market stability objective emerged in response to banking unrest. Since the leading New York bankers also served as part-time officials of the Clearing House, there existed an ongoing institutional arrangement for fostering cooperation and collective action among the members on matters other than the clearing and collecting of checks.

To conserve the supply of cash among the member banks the Clearing House was authorized to allow petitioning banks to issue clearing house certificates. To be able to meet the cash withdrawals of out-of-town banks it also had the power to equalize or pool the reserves of the associated banks. In specific cases funds could be made available directly to troubled banks. The Clearing House Committee of the NYCH assumed responsibility for examining and assisting banks whose solvency was questioned by unfavorable rumors. When the bank was found to be solvent, a public statement was issued to that effect. If the bank was "hopelessly insolvent," it was removed as a member of the Clearing House. Between December 1871 and October 1907 at least sixteen banks were examined: fifteen were declared solvent and one insolvent. Where necessary, aid was extended by some members of the Clearing House, their losses, if any, being covered by the NYCH. In the event all else failed, the NYCH suspended cash payment. The power that the Clearing House possessed was impressive even in the absence of authority to vary the amount of the legal tender reserve provided that the size of the reserve was satisfactory.

Both the size and distribution of the banking reserve among the New York banks was conducive to the recognition of the special role played by New York banks in the maintenance of banking stability. The ultimate banking reserves of the country were lodged in six or seven of the largest of the New York banks. The size of those reserves according to Sprague was greater than that held by any one of Europe's central banks. Learning how to manage those reserves was the chief task of the NYCH during the national banking era. To be specific: Could a purely voluntary association of private banks learn how to manage successfully those reserves to maintain banking stability in the absence of a central bank? The response of the NYCH to the banking panics between the Civil War and World War I should provide answers to that question.

Successful management did not necessarily mean having the instruments to alter the size of the banking reserve. The problem as we intend to show was the distribution of those reserves among the member banks of the Clearing House. In particular it was the distribution of those reserves among the six or seven New York banks holding the bulk of the deposits of the interior banks. The NYCH had the authority whenever it deemed necessary to equalize or pool the reserves of the clearing house banks. The Clearing House assumed control over the reserves of the member banks by transferring funds from banks with surplus cash to banks with a cash deficiency, thereby tending to forestall the suspension of cash payment. Reserve pooling had been used on two previous occasions in 1860 and 1861 before the NYCH authorized its use during the panic of 1873. Nevertheless, it suspended cash payment even though it continued to pay out cash freely to interior banks.

The significance of reserve pooling was clearly understood by a special clearing house committee headed by George S. Coe. The committee issued a report in November 1873 and effectively made the case that banking panics could be averted if the NYCH exercised bold leadership and was fully prepared to use its power and instruments to achieve its objective. How, then, do we explain the failure of the NYCH to equalize reserves in subsequent panics? Opposition within the Clearing House was not great though it was capable of thwarting the will of the majority.

Conventional wisdom has attributed the banking panics of the national banking era to special historical circumstances: structural weaknesses of the national banking system in conjunction with a seasonal flow of funds between New York and the South and West, mainly at crop moving time. But a more fundamental cause may have played a dominant role: institutional failure. The NYCH may not have been an effective institution for crafting a policy of collective action. Another way of expressing the same point is that NYCH policy was not incentive compatible. The self-interest of the separate banks was incompatible with voluntary collective action.

Critical delays in responding to the onset of banking unrest in 1893 and 1907 exacerbated the panic's symptoms. These delays can be attributable to an unduly narrow conception of the NYCH's responsibilities. The Clearing House was hesitant at first about accepting responsibility for the banking panic of 1893, which originated outside New York. Only after massive withdrawals of interior banks did the NYCH authorize the issue of loan certificates. In 1907 the delay in Clearing House action arose from a reluctance to extend support to the troubled trust companies who were not members of the Clearing House association. By failing to respond quickly enough, leadership passed to J. P. Morgan, who resorted to the use of "money pools" to contain the panic.

It is clear that considerations of self-interest marred the behavior of the NYCH in 1893 and 1907. The origin of these two panics bore little resemblance to earlier panic episodes: Its origin in 1893 was outside New York and the 1907 panic originated with the trust companies. The self-interest of the Clearing House was definitely paramount. There was less concern for banks outside the Clearing House and for banks in the interior. The NYCH was never able except in 1860, 1861, and 1873 to make the transition effectively accomplished by the Bank of England after Bagehot. Neither for that matter did the Federal Reserve. Federal Reserve officials were more concerned about banking stability in New York than they were about banking stability in the rest of the country during the Great Depression. How else can we explain their reluctance to intervene to moderate the banking panics of 1930 and 1931?

The NYCH had the potential for preventing banking panics, or at least moderating their effects; it had the power and the instruments but simply could not craft a successful policy of voluntary action.

Summary

The construction of reliable estimates of the number of bank failures in both the central money market and the interior is the first step in understanding what happened during banking panics. They fill a notorious gap in our knowledge without which we are not able to assess the relative impact of the different panics. However, numbers alone do not tell the full story. They need to be supplemented by deposits in failed banks as well as information on the incidence of bank runs, when available.

Our single most important finding from the bank suspension evidence, surprisingly perhaps, is the smallness of their numbers especially when compared with the banking panics of the Great Depression. The average number of bank failures for each panic exempting 1893 is less than 100, whereas for the Great Depression it was over 700! The average is even smaller when we adjust for the failure of private banks (brokerage houses).

It seems clear that the number of bank suspensions is a poor indicator of how banking panics affected the interior. The average person living in the interior had little direct experience of bank runs and bank closings. The response of the interior was more closely identified with the suspension of cash payment: hoarding increased, payroll delinquencies emerged, and the real cost of transactions increased. These alleged difficulties were not always discernible in the broad annual real GNP and unemployment estimates except in 1893 and 1907. The New York Clearing House had the knowledge, the power, and the instruments to forestall banking panics. But apparently that was not enough. Considerations of self-interest could not be reconciled with an effective policy of voluntary collective action. Institutional failure rather than structural weaknesses of the national baking system and seasonal flows of funds explain the frequency of banking panics of the national banking era.

2 The Banking Panic of 1873

The 1873 panic was the first of the banking panics of the national banking era. The fact that it occurred after the passage of the National Banking Act in 1863 is not of as much significance as the response of the New York Clearing House. For a brief interval between 1860 and 1873 the NYCH possessed vigorous leadership. George S. Coe, President of the American Exchange Bank, understood the broader responsibilities of the NYCH as holder of the country's ultimate banking reserve and designer of the two powerful instruments for forestalling banking panics: loan certificates and the pooling of reserves of the associated banks; the loan certificate enabled the member banks to expand loans during the panic episode without the loss of reserves to local banks, and reserve pooling allowed the banks to continue to pay out cash freely to the interior banks. The significance of reserve pooling was recognized by Sprague (1910), who argued correctly that it effectively converted the NYCH into a central bank with reserve power greater than that of any European central bank. Although the NYCH suspended cash payment, it continued to pay out cash freely to interior banks, thereby moderating the effects of the panic. As we see below the suspension of cash payment was probably unnecessary, but, given the knowledge available, understandable. For reasons to be spelled out later, reserve pooling was not repeated in future panics, and by 1893 and 1907 that knowledge had completely evaporated from the collective memory of the NYCH.

The resumption of specie payment was some six years away, thus ruling out gold imports as a device for replenishing the public's holdings of cash. Nevertheless, gold could still be used to meet reserve requirements.

Banking disturbances in 1873 were not confined to the United States. According to Schumpeter (1939, vol. 1, p. 335) the European crisis had its origin in Vienna where the stock market collapsed in May; there were, however, no immediate effects outside Austria-Hungary. Speaking metaphorically Schumpeter stated: "The American scaffolding received its first decisive shock on the wire of foreign credit." Glassner (1997, p. 133) identified the shock as a crisis of confidence of European investors who sought to liquidate their holdings of American securities. The full impact was delayed until the advent of the crop moving season in August and early September. After the panic had subsided in the United States, the Vienna stock exchange crashed again, spreading its effects to other European capitals when railway stocks and railway finance became focal points of the banking crisis.

In the first section I provide original estimates of the number and geographical incidence of bank suspensions followed in the second section by an extensive narrative of bank runs and bank closings in specific cities and towns. In the third section I attempt to identify the purely financial effects of the panic, and in the fourth section I examine what the evidence tells us about the real effects, that is, real GNP and unemployment. The fifth describes the response of the New York Clearing House.

Bank Suspension Estimates

Our first task is to describe what happened during the banking panic to the number and incidence of bank suspensions. There are no estimates of total bank closures during the panic month of September 1873. The Comptroller of the Currency listed national bank suspensions and receiverships in his *Annual Report*; he also attempted to obtain data on state, private, and savings banks. Legislation in 1873 required the Comptroller to report on the resources and liabilities of banking companies not otherwise the responsibility of the Comptroller. He had to admit that he was not able to obtain usable information on state, private, and savings banks. Of the thirty-seven states where the information was requested, only eight responded to his inquiry and there were no responses at all from the nine territories. We have a fairly complete record of what happened in New York City but little or no knowledge about the course of the banking panic in the interior.

My estimates have been constructed from two principal sources: contemporary newspaper accounts where banking disturbances occurred and contemporary financial journals, including *Bradstreet's* and the *Commercial and Financial Chronicle*. I make no claim that my estimates include all bank failures that occurred in the United States during the panic month, but every effort was made to check and cross-check claims that specific banks had shut down even if only temporarily. These estimates do provide a reliable guide to the geographical incidence and numbers of bank suspensions.

Table 2.1. *Bank suspensions New York and interior by type of bank organization, September 1873*

	National	State	Savings	Private	Trust	Unclassified	Total
New York	1			34	2		37
Interior	15	11	7	25	2	4	64
Total	16	11	7	59	4	4	101

The wave of bank suspensions in the interior followed the suspension of cash payments in New York on September 24. Table 2.1 shows bank suspensions in New York and the interior separately by bank classification, that is, national, state, private, and savings banks, and trust companies.

Two things stand out very clearly from the table: the extremely small number of bank suspensions, excluding brokerage houses, in New York – one national bank and two trust companies – and the high percentage of suspensions among private banks or brokerage houses. Nearly 60 percent of all bank suspensions were brokerage houses and not conventional commercial banks; for the interior the percentage was smaller (39%), of which at least one-half were in Philadelphia. Considering that there were fewer than forty bank suspensions in the country as a whole, excluding brokerage firms, would suggest that bank suspensions as a principal characteristic of banking panics has been perhaps greatly exaggerated. We should look elsewhere for the main impact of a banking disturbance.

The geographical incidence of bank failures during the 1873 banking panic is shown in Table 2.2. The highest concentration of closures was in three states: New York, Pennsylvania, and Virginia, with over 70 percent of all bank suspensions. The Middle Atlantic region accounted for 60 percent, due almost entirely to the collapse of forty-five brokerage houses in New York and Philadelphia. The Southern and Midwestern states each accounted for 20 percent.

The bank suspension data understate the amount of banking unrest, for they fail to reveal the prevalence of bank runs that did not result in any bank closures. For example, there were serious city-wide runs in Augusta and Savannah, Georgia; Louisville, Kentucky; Charleston, South Carolina; Nashville and Knoxville, Tennessee; and Petersburg and Richmond, Virginia.

Table 2.2. *Bank suspensions by state and grouped by region, September 1873*

Middle Atlantic	
New York	37
Pennsylvania	22
Southern	
Virginia	10
Washington, D.C.	2
Georgia ⎱	
Alabama ⎬	7
Tennessee ⎰	
Midwest	
Illinois	8
Ohio	4
Wisconsin ⎱	
Iowa ⎬	7
Michigan ⎰	
Other regions	4
Total	101

Source: Author's estimates.

Our second task is to provide a detailed narrative of the panic as experienced in New York and the interior.

Banking Panic Narrative

The Brooklyn Trust Co. closed its doors in July 1873 with apparently no ill effects; it had made advances to the New Haven and Willimantic railroad. But to the few that were prescient the collapse of the company should have been a subtle harbinger of what was to follow. The unsatisfactory financial condition of the railroads brought on by their last-minute efforts to obtain temporary financial accommodation at private banks (brokerage houses) made these banks especially vulnerable to liquidity shocks. The underlying cause of this predicament was the reckless attempt to expand railway mileage prematurely into the undeveloped Western territory.

The Mercantile Warehouse and Security company failed on September 8, followed by the closure of Kenyon, Cox and Co. on September 13. The first had advanced funds on the bonds of the Missouri, Kansas and Texas Railroad and was unable to meet the interest payments, and the second had endorsed $1 million of paper of the Canada Southern Railroad which fell due September 15. But the shock that gained both national and international attention was the failure of Jay Cooke and Co. on September 18; the Philadelphia branch had made a $15 million advance to the Northern Pacific Railroad for construction credit. The First National Bank in Philadelphia, wholly owned by Cooke's and E. C. Clark and Company, suspended, and the First National Bank of Washington, D.C., also a Cooke enterprise, failed to open with $2.5 million of assets.

Jay Cooke and Co. was one of the most prestigious merchant banking houses in the United States. Its closing was a surprise and changed the character of the crisis. Although it was not the first of the private banks in New York to fail, the news that its affiliates in Philadelphia and Washington, D.C., including the First National Bank of Washington, D.C., had also closed brought pandemonium to Wall Street. Stock prices tumbled, followed by a veritable wave of insolvencies, including more than thirty brokerage houses.

There were "slight runs" on two Washington banks: Freedman's Bank and the Washington, D.C., Savings Bank, which was forced to close a week later. The runs on the two Philadelphia banks were bank-specific. The runs on the Fidelity Trust and Safety Deposit Bank and the Union Banking Co. were sizable and continuous. There were large lines of frantic depositors awaiting their turns to withdraw deposits along with others who were merely curious onlookers, all of whom contributed to the excitement and uncertainty that prevailed. Their numbers were large enough to require police surveillance to insure that order was maintained. Fidelity Trust survived but Union Trust failed. Eleven brokerage houses were also victims of the Philadelphia crisis. The *Philadelphia Enquirer* (September 23) conjectured on the basis of what evidence we do not know that depositors had withdrawn $30 million during the first three days of banking unrest in the three cities of New York, Philadelphia, and Washington, D.C.

According to Henrietta Larson, Cooke's biographer (1968, p. 410), the firm was overloaded with investments and advances made to specific railroads, including Northern Pacific and Lake Superior and Mississippi. Credit stringency made it impossible to obtain funds to tide it over until the panic assuaged. She maintained that Jay Cooke marked the close of an important phase of American business; that is, "the speculative promotion of railroads beyond a reasonable expectation of returns under the drive of post-war conditions."

The next day after the announcement of Cooke's failure, the banker and brokerage firm of Fisk and Hatch suspended. Runs began immediately on two New York banks: Union Trust and Fourth National, the latter having deposits of $17 million, one-half of which represented the deposits of other banks. The National Bank of Commonwealth, with deposits of $1.7 million; National Trust; and Union Trust suspended on the 20th. On the 23rd a run began on all the savings banks in New York City and in Brooklyn. The two trust companies resumed normal operations, one as early as October 15, the other in December.

The Commonwealth Bank had overdrawn its account at the NYCH by $200,000, and Union Trust could not retrieve its call loans; moreover, there was a defalcation by its secretary involving the sum of $500,000. There had been heavy withdrawals from the National Bank of Commonwealth in December 1871 due to unfavorable rumors. The NYCH Committee met on that occasion, examined its condition, and concluded that it was "perfectly solvent" (NYCH Committee Minutes, December 14, 1871). The Union Bank of Philadelphia closed on the 20th, precipitating the suspension of the Keystone Bank, Citizen's Bank, and State Bank. By the time the panic in New York had subsided, more than thirty-two brokerage firms had gone under.

The intensity of the panic in the stock market forced its closing for ten days, ending September 30, the first time in its history. The NYCH Committee voted on September 20 to authorize the issue of clearing house loan certificates. Also the Clearing House voted to equalize the reserves of the NYCH banks; it gave the Clearing House the authority to redistribute the currency reserves of the individual banks, a measure which should have avoided the suspension of cash payment. Sprague (1910, p. 90) described the significance of the measure in these terms:

During the continuance of this arrangement banks were converted to all intents and purposes, into a central bank, which, although without power to issue notes, was in other respects more powerful than a European central bank, because it included virtually all the banking power in the city.

Nevertheless, the overall reserve position of the New York banks became so desperate, or so it was thought, that partial suspension became unavoidable. The NYCH partially suspended cash payments on September 24, which by the 27th had been extended to the rest of the country.

From September 18 to 26 banking unrest spread selectively down the Eastern seaboard, from New York, Philadelphia, and Washington, D.C., to Petersburg and Richmond, Virginia; Augusta and Savannah, Georgia; and Charleston, South Carolina. Simultaneously banking disturbances erupted in the middle of the country: in Memphis, Indianapolis, Chicago, and Louisville. The residue of so much banking turmoil was bank runs, bank closures, and restrictions on cash payment by some troubled banks. Nevertheless, what is perhaps most surprising is the small number of cities that bore the full impact of the banking panic. Our narrative of the course of the banking panic will begin with what happened along the Eastern seaboard and then shift to mid-continent, where events in Chicago overshadow banking unrest elsewhere.

The banking situation at the time of suspension was described by Sprague (1910, pp. 67–8) as follows:

Up to the time of suspension there had been no failures of consequence in general business, and no failures of banks outside New York, except those in Philadelphia and Washington, in connection with the failure of Jay Cooke and Co. Confidence in the banks had not been seriously weakened, and there were few reports of runs and hoarding by individuals outside New York. . . . *there was no further panic during 1873*, though the crisis had only begun and although the effects of suspension which had been brought about by the panic had yet to be experienced. [emphasis added]

Sprague simply overlooked what was happening in the interior. The banking panic in the interior began on the day preceding the partial suspension of cash payments in New York. The initial damage had been confined to the three cities of New York, Washington, and Philadelphia. By the time the panic had moderated, over fifty brokerage houses had failed in New York and Philadelphia. The collapse of so many brokerage firms was directly or indirectly connected with the stock market panic, but on a deeper level involvement in the financing of railroad construction was at the root of the problem.

The panic spread to Petersburg, Virginia, on September 23. There were serious runs on all but one of Petersburg's nine banks. Two of the national banks – Merchant's National and First National – were declared insolvent and receivers appointed by the Comptroller of the Currency. On the October call date in 1872 Merchant's National had individual deposits of $610,000, and First National $177,000. People's and Planters and Mechanic's banks also closed. People's bank was solvent and resumed normal operations on October 4. The Citizen's Saving Bank closed the next day, September 24. The Commercial National Bank and Petersburg Savings and Insurance Co. endured heavy runs but remained open. Only one bank, the Bank of Petersburg, escaped the run. We do not know whether there was any connection between the failure of Jay Cooke's branch in Washington, D.C., and any of the Petersburg banks. But the proximity to Washington and the events there could very plausibly have inspired the banking unrest in Petersburg. That, however, is only a conjecture.

When the news of the Petersburg banking unrest reached Richmond, Virginia, on September 24 there was a steady stream of withdrawals but no general run on all of the banks. The heaviest drains occurred at the two banks with alleged close relationships with the Petersburg banks. Two banks failed: Dollar Savings Bank and Mutual Loan Co., which paid out its last dollar before closing, and Isaac, Taylor, Williams, a private bank; it had been subjected to unusually heavy demands during the past four days. The Lancaster Bank failed on the 25th, and the Freedman's Saving Bank required notice for withdrawal. The officers of the national banks in Richmond met on the 24th and agreed to stand by each other if the need arose. On the 26th, however, the Richmond Clearing House agreed to the issue of loan certificates to settle interbank claims. The panic in Richmond subsided.

Banking unrest spread to Augusta, Georgia, on the 25th. The local paper, the *Daily Constitutionalist*, reported that three of the city's banks had "succumbed." These included Merchant's and Planters National Bank, and Planters Loan and Savings Bank, the latter two of which shared the same president. "Succumbed" apparently referred to the suspension of cash payment rather than closure, for Merchant's and Planters resumed payment to small depositors on the 29th. Three more banks suspended payment temporarily. All of the banks, however, were solvent.

From Augusta, Georgia, the loss of depositor confidence engulfed the contiguous cities of Savannah and Charleston, South Carolina, though the transmission mechanism is unclear. On Friday, September 26, runs occurred on three banks in Savannah including the Savannah Bank and Trust Co. and the Southern Bank of the State of Georgia. Three banks in Charleston suspended payment "without excitement and no failures."

Between September 23 and September 26, banking unrest moved quickly down the Atlantic Coast from Petersburg, Virginia to Savannah Georgia. There were eight bank failures, six banks that suspended cash payment temporarily, and runs on at least eleven or more banks. The banking disturbance was not general being confined to no more than five cities.

The reaction in Chicago to the failure of Jay Cooke on September 18 was immediate. Real estate and grain prices plunged. The brokerage firm of A. C. and O. F. Badger failed, followed on the 20th by the closing of the Franklin Bank due to its inability to meet indebtedness to the Clearing House. Fifteen out of twenty savings banks required notice for deposit withdrawal. During the next four days no more banks suspended but Chicago banks began to withdraw large balances from New York.

James's (1938) description of Chicago on the eve of the banking panic revealed that the city was rapidly becoming a reserve center, second only to New York in the holding of bankers' balances. It did not, however, equal Boston and Philadelphia in total bank resources. Nevertheless, the description of banking instability in Chicago had the potential for diffusing depositor uncertainty throughout the Midwest.

The NYCH had announced on the 24th the suspension of cash payment. The response of the Chicago Clearing House was immediate. A meeting of the Clearing House that same evening could reach no agreement about either the authorization to issue loan certificates or the equalization of reserves. The motion was defeated by a vote of 11 to 8.

By refusing to follow the lead of New York in authorizing loan certificates and the equalization of reserves despite the suspension of cash payment in other large cities, the members revealed a wide disparity of opinion among the bankers themselves about what appropriate action to take. To some, to continue to pay out currency when banks in other important cities had refused was not a viable policy since there was no way to replace the depleted reserves. But they did take the unprecedented step of recommending that the members at their discretion could suspend cash payments "on any large demands made upon them either from country banks or over their counters."

Not all of the Chicago banks responded to the Clearing House offer. The few that did not were caught up in serious bank runs that erupted on September 26. Five national banks closed including Union National, the largest bank in the West, with nearly $4 million of deposits; three-fourths of its deposits were due to other banks and constituted one-third of the bankers' balances held by Chicago banks. The impact of this closure cannot be overestimated. This fact alone is sufficient to explain how fear and uncertainty could have spread throughout the Midwest. Other national bank suspensions with deposit totals include: Cook County National Bank, $1.5 million; Second National Bank, $650,000; Manufacturers' National Bank, $1.5 million; and National Bank of Commerce, $800,000.

On the 29th, the Third National Bank failed with deposits of $2.9 million, for a grand total of deposits in failed banks in Chicago of $9.6 million, or approximately 25 percent of the total deposits of national banks in the city. The suspension of the six largest national banks produced serious runs on all the other banks in Chicago. Nevertheless, the suspensions were temporary; all reopened on the 29th with the single exception of the Union National which reopened on October 14. All of the closed national banks were solvent.

Select balance sheet items for national banks in Chicago between September 12 and October 13 are shown below:

	September 12	October 13
Loans and discounts	$25.3 million	$14.4 million
Due from reserve agents	3.6	1.6
Legal tender notes	5.1	5.3
Specie	0.1	0.1
Deposits	17.4	13.5

Loans and discounts contracted by more than 40 percent and deposits by 22 percent. Legal tender notes and specie (reserves) hardly changed! Why? Chicago banks retrieved bankers' balances from New York to meet their withdrawal needs. Otherwise they hoarded cash, the same as the country banks. James (1938, p. 454) concluded: "Such a credit contraction reinforced by hoarding of currency on the part of most of the banks, could not fail to accentuate the crisis in the local market. . . . Such a policy . . . is contrary to every canon of banking theory." But to James out of this debacle the banks of Chicago learned a new sense of responsibility: "The panic, in a sense, constituted the birth pains of the central reserve city that was soon to arise" (p. 455).

Memphis, like Chicago, continued cash payment after the New York banks suspended payment on September 24. A run without parallel in Memphis history began the same day with large deposit withdrawals at the First National Bank; it was forced to close on the 25th. The *Memphis Daily Appeal* conjectured that 15,000 to 20,000 panic-stricken depositors withdrew $1 million. The First National Bank was probably solvent, for it resumed normal operations on October 2. The DeSota and the Freedman's Savings Bank also closed.

The banking unrest spread to Indianapolis and Louisville. Woolen, Webb and Co. of Indianapolis with deposits of approximately $500,000 suspended operations on the 25th; a quarter of its deposits were deposits of country banks. It reopened almost immediately upon the receipt of $50,000 from other banks in the city. The next day there was a sizable run on Ritzinger's Bank and slight runs on a few other banks: Fletcher and Sharp and Citizens National. The Indianapolis Clearing House voted to limit payment to depositors on the 26th.

After the morning edition of the *Louisville Courier Journal* on September 27 announced in blatant terms that there was not the slightest sign of panic in Louisville, a panic had engulfed the financial district. Seven German savings banks simply refused to cash checks and thereby suspended payment temporarily; the decision to stop payment had been made the previous evening. Apparently unknown to the newspaper reporters, these banks had been subject to steady withdrawals since the previous Monday. A "silent" run had begun which the reporters had failed to detect. All banks in Louisville were subjected to withdrawals on Saturday. The response of the presidents and chief bank officers when they met to consider the banking situation was to suspend cash payment with payment to resume in thirty days.

There certainly were no widespread banking disturbances in the interior during the 1873 panic. Suspensions were few, confined mainly to the South and Midwest.

The Panic's Impact: The Financial Effects

Measures of the financial impact of the 1873 panic are part of what I have referred to as the information deficit about what happened in the interior. We really do not know, for example, how the money stock behaved. Friedman and Schwartz (1963) constructed annual estimates (February 1873 to February 1974) of M1 (currency and demand deposits) and M2 (currency and demand and time deposits) which revealed a 1.8 percent decline in M1 and an increase of 1.3 percent in M2. Their monthly estimates begin only in May 1907. Unlike the banking panics of the Great Depression it is quite clear that bank failures per se did not cause a contraction of M (the money stock) because of the fewness of their numbers.

Nor do we have any direct estimates of the amount of hoarding. The impact of the September crisis is not easy to discern because the effects of banking panics, if any, are intertwined with the normal seasonal outflows of funds from New York. We might have reasonably expected an increase in hoarding, if not before, at least after the partial suspension of cash payments. Partial suspension induced the substitution of cash for check payments, and the currency premium reflected a scramble for cash. Between September 12 and October 13 legal tender notes held by national banks declined by more than 25 percent. But by November 1, one-half of that loss had been recovered. Sprague conjectured (1910, p. 70) that no considerable amount of money lost by the banks was then being hoarded by depositors because of the normal seasonal demands of the crop moving season.

The extent of money market stringency is revealed in Table 2.3, which shows monthly commercial paper rates in New York; rates soared in September and October, increasing by over 136 percent! Call money rates suffered even wilder gyrations.

The monthly behavior of stock prices is given in Table 2.4. The intensity of the stock market panic is revealed by the 8.8 percent decline between August and September and a 19.8 percent decline between

Table 2.3. *Prime commercial paper rates in New York, 1873*

January	9.40
February	9.15
March	10.10
April	10.75
May	8.20
June	6.80
July	6.50
August	7.20
September	12.50
October	17.00
November	13.85
December	10.15

Source: Crum, 1923.

Table 2.4. *Cowles Commission all stocks price index,* 1873

January	40.4
February	40.8
March	40.4
April	39.7
May	39.9
June	39.4
July	39.3
August	39.8
September	36.3
October	33.1
November	31.9
December	34.9

Source: Alfred Cowles et al., 1938.
* July 1926 = 100.

August and November. The monthly figures mute the extent of the daily decline. The stock market for the first time in its history was forced to close for ten days, reopening on September 30.

Our most reliable source of information on the financial effects of the panic is the balance sheets of the national banks on the various call dates

Table 2.5. *Changes in loans and discounts, total deposits, and legal tender currency at national bank call dates, 1871–1873 (in millions of dollars)*

	Loans and discounts	Total deposits	Legal tender
1871 (June 10–Oct. 2)	42.2	13.5	–12.7
1872 (June 10–Oct. 3)	5.7	–5.5	–17.9
1873 (June 13–Oct. 13)	–124.5	–126.2	–24.9

Source: Annual Reports of the Comptroller of the Currency, Washington, D.C.

of the Comptroller of the Currency. Loans, deposits, and reserves of the national banks are a good indicator of what was happening in the banking system as a whole. In 1870 the number of state banks and their assets amounted to less than 10 percent of the total. In 1880 the proportion had risen to almost 30 percent. The number of state banks did not overtake the number of national banks until sometime between 1890 and 1900.

Table 2.5 shows changes in loans and discounts, total deposits, and legal tender currency at comparable call dates between 1871 and 1873. Both loan and deposit contraction were substantial in 1873 relative to comparable call dates in the two previous years. Legal tender holdings were nearly 40 percent less than in 1872. Data in Table 2.5 on the behavior of changes in legal tender currency do not warrant our ruling out Sprague's conjecture that no considerable amount of money lost by the banks was being hoarded by depositors because of the normal seasonal demands associated with the movement of crops. The increase in the percentage change between 1872 and 1873 was about the same as between 1871 and 1872 when there was no banking panic.

Loan and deposit contraction was not uniform among the several states. Approximately 40 percent of the loan contraction occurred in the three middle Atlantic states: New York, New Jersey, and Pennsylvania; 23 percent in the three Midwestern states: Ohio, Indiana, and Illinois; and 15 percent in Massachusetts and Connecticut. Three-fourths of all the loan contraction of national banks between September 12 and October 13 was concentrated in these eight states. Sixty percent of total deposit contraction occurred in the same eight states, one-half of which was attributable to New York, New Jersey, and Pennsylvania.

Table 2.6 shows changes in loans and deposits between September 12 and October 13 for country, reserve city, and New York banks. New York

Table 2.6. *Changes in loans and total deposits between September 12 and October 13 for country, reserve city, and New York banks (in millions of dollars)*

	Loans and discounts	Total deposits
Country	−23	−45
Reserve city	−15	−27
New York City	−20	−37

was the only central reserve city. The impact of the panic in the interior as measured by loan and deposit contraction of national banks was twice what it was in New York, contraction being the more severe among the country banks.

Country and Reserve City banks responded to the panic by drawing down their reserves with reserve agents by $42 million. New York City banks shipped $14.5 million of legal tender notes to the interior and due to other banks declined by $34.9 million. Although the number of suspensions in the interior was not large and was specific to a small number of cities and towns, there was a substantial flow of funds from New York to interior banks as measured solely by the balance sheets of the national banks. After the middle of October, currency began to flow back into the New York banks.

The Panic's Impact: The Real Effects

According to business cycle annals a serious cyclical contraction followed the panic in September 1873. The National Bureau of Economic Research identified the cyclical peak in October 1873, making it appear plausible that the panic in the preceding month was a proximate cause of the contraction which followed. Fels (1959, p. 98) opted for September as the cyclical peak but did not rule out the possibility that the expansion might have leveled off before the panic. If not the cause, the panic at the very least exacerbated the downturn.

In the absence of estimates of real GNP Sprague had to be content with proxy measures of the real effects: disruption of the domestic exchanges, delays in the transshipment of commodities to the East, and payroll difficulties. Qualitative indicators were a substitute for more precise quantitative measures. But that is no longer the case. We now

Table 2.7. *Behavior of the Romer and Balke-Gordon real GNP and price deflator estimates, 1869–1875*

| | Real GNP ($ billion) | | Price deflator (1982 = 100) | |
	Romer	Balke-Gordon	Romer	Balke-Gordon
1869	75.609	78.2	10.244	10.49
1870	76.464	84.2	9.661	9.98
1871	76.952	88.1	9.769	9.86
1872	89.605	91.7	9.423	9.60
1873	94.863	96.3	9.329	9.51
1874	96.205	95.7	9.169	9.25
1875	97.684	100.7	8.945	8.85
1876	104.628	101.9	8.539	8.51
1877	110.797	105.2	8.207	8.38
1878	118.906	109.6	7.627	7.87
1879	127.675	123.1	7.378	7.64

Source: Romer, 1989, p. 84; Balke and Gordon, 1989, p. 84.

have two separate annual estimates of real GNP and the GNP price deflator for the years 1869–1929 constructed by Romer (1989) and Balke and Gordon (1989), shown in Table 2.7. There was no decline in real GNP in either the panic or post-panic year in Romer's estimates and a slight fall of a little more than one-half percent in the post-panic year in Balke-Gordon. Although Romer found no decline in 1874, there was a sharp falloff in the rate of increase.

The decline in the GNP price deflator was continuous from 1869 to 1875 with the single exception of 1871 in Romer's index. The Balke-Gordon index showed no interruption in the price decline. The Romer index decreased by 12.7 percent and the Balke-Gordon 15.6 percent. During the same interval (1869–75) real GNP increased 29 percent for both indices, but the rate of increase was much greater between 1869 and 1872 than between 1872 and 1875: 18 percent in the earlier period and only 9 percent in the latter. After 1873 the growth rate was much slower: only 3 percent in Romer and 4.6 percent in Balke-Gordon.

Contemporary accounts describe the post-panic years of contraction as years of almost unrelieved gloom. But the evidence for such gloom is certainly not apparent in the Romer-Balke-Gordon estimates of real GNP. It was obvious to Fels, even before the new estimates became available, that output contraction had been mild; he cited the fact that manufacturing output did not decline after 1875 and the fact that real per capita income was one-third greater in 1879 than ten years earlier.

Our information deficit is formidable with respect to unemployment. Lebergott's estimates begin in 1890 and Romer's (1986) revised estimates begin in the same year. Schumpeter (1939, p. 337) claimed that unemployment became more serious almost immediately after the onset of the 1873 panic, but he provided no evidence to support his claim of three million unemployed. Fels (1959, p. 198) thought such figures gave a "a greatly exaggerated impression." He cited Carroll Wright's (1879) estimate of 28,500 unemployed in Massachusetts in a labor force of 318,000, or roughly 8.9 percent. Wright simply applied the ratio in Massachusetts to the whole country and came up with an overall unemployment in the United States at 570,000. See the Appendix for a review of Wright's estimates.

Without more reliable unemployment estimates, there is no way to assess the basis for the alleged perception of unrelieved gloom or a favorable comparison with the depressions of the 1890s with the 1930s. There was, however, a basis for gloom in the agricultural sector where persistently falling commodity prices drastically reduced agricultural income. Moreover, declining prices increased the burden of mortgage indebtedness and railway freight rates did not fall as rapidly as the prices of the major crops, thereby generating a cost-price squeeze. Farmers' unrest is attested by the growth of pressure groups such as the Grange, and the increased political activity was evidenced by the formation of the Greenback party in 1875, whose major objective was currency expansion.

The Response of the New York Clearing House

The NYCH responded to the 1873 panic as it had done in the banking disturbances in 1860 and 1861, that is, by authorizing the issue of loan certificates and the equalization of reserves among the member banks. Nevertheless, cash payment was partially suspended in 1873 and not in the earlier episodes. The equalization of reserves, however, enabled the seven large New York banks that held the bulk of bankers' balances to continue to pay out cash freely to interior banks. Why, then, did reserve equalization fail to prevent the suspension of cash payments in 1873? Sprague conjectured that the New York banks held an inadequate level of reserves prior to the panic. The clearing house banks held only $53.2 million of total reserves immediately prior to suspension on September 24. Since specie did not circulate, the relevant component of total reserves was legal tender currency and that showed (Table 2.8) a decrease of $13 million from the previous week, or a 38 percent decline.

Table 2.8. *Legal tender reserves of NYCH banks, September 20 to October 24, 1873 (in millions of dollars)*

September 20	33.8
24	15.8
25	14.9
26	14.1
27	12.3
29	10.1
30	9.3
October 1	8.3
2	7.7
3	7.2
4	6.9
7	5.9
8	6.5
9	6.8
10	6.6
11	6.5
13	6.0
14	5.8
15	6.2
16	6.1
17	6.6
18	7.0
20	6.8
21	7.7
22	8.4
23	9.4
24	9.9

Source: NYCH Loan Committee, Minutes, December 2, 1861 to January 8, 1874, p. 24.

The proportion of reserves to deposits had fallen from 23 to 16.97 percent. Sprague (1910, p. 54) concluded: "The banks were clearly at the end of their resources, and the step taken on Wednesday, September 24, seems amply justified." But was it? What is clear is that the NYCH banks continued to pay out currency to interior banks almost as freely as before suspension, as is evident from Table 2.8. Legal tender currency had fallen to an all-time low of only \$5.8 million on October 14. Considering the extent to which they were prepared to go on paying out currency after suspension, we can well wonder why cash payment was suspended. The equalization of reserves was what made possible the ultra-liberal policy of continuing to pay out cash to the interior, which we do not observe in future panics. Since the suspension of cash payment was always accompanied by an increase in hoarding, the actual level of the legal tender reserve *after suspension* probably overstates what the level would have been in the absence of suspension. There was really no economic necessity for the suspension of cash payment.

The first post–Civil War banking panic did not uncover any evidence that a large number of banks in New York and the interior were in a prior troubled state. With the exception of a few banks and some brokerage houses, the general condition of the banks was good. Banking unrest in the interior was greatest in Philadelphia and Chicago. The loss of depositor confidence was perhaps more general, being expressed in the form of "silent" withdrawals rather than the more sensational bank runs and bank closures. Equally important was the panic-like response of the interior banks who amidst the excitement made large withdrawals of their balances from New York, presumably to meet unexpected deposit withdrawals, but more likely it was simply the result of fear and uncertainty about the availability of their New York balances. Reserves fell to critically low levels only after the suspension of cash payment and after reserves had been equalized.

The New York banks behaved responsibly after the suspension of cash payment by continuing to pay out cash freely to interior banks, thereby minimizing the adverse effects of suspension. We can fault the NYCH for having suspended cash payment; it was unnecessary. Suspension exacerbated the amount of hoarding. We can speculate that had payment not been suspended reserves would not have fallen so precipitously, and the country banks would have had less reason for withdrawing their New York balances. Inexperience as well as a knowledge deficit explain the response of the NYCH.

3 The Incipient Banking Panics of 1884 and 1890: An Unheralded Success Story

The banking disturbances in 1884 and 1890 do not resemble the banking panics of 1873, 1893, and 1907 in at least four important aspects. The number of bank closings excluding brokerage houses (private banks) in both New York and the interior were few, probably not more than twenty in each episode. The prompt action by the NYCH in coming to the aid of the distressed banks by authorizing the issue of clearing house loan certificates was responsible for preventing the banking difficulties in New York from worsening and from spreading to the interior. In neither episode was there a general loss of depositor confidence either in New York or in the rest of the country. Failures for the most part were bank-specific, having as their cause, real or alleged, the misappropriation of funds or careless and imprudent management practices rather than a contagion of fear overtaking solvent and insolvent banks alike. More-over, there was no suspension of cash payment.

The action of the NYCH was able to contain the banking disturbances in 1884 and 1890 in an incipient stage and thereby halt any escalation into a full-scale banking panic. A better understanding of what happened in these two periods may provide useful insight into why the banking panics of '73, '93, and 1907 were far more serious as measured by the number and incidence of bank closings, the amount of hoarding, and the effects on the rest of the country.

This chapter is divided into two parts. In the first we attempt to describe what happened during the banking disturbance of 1884: esti-mate the number of bank closings; provide a chronology of events during the peak panic month of May; show the behavior of loans, deposits, and surplus reserves of the NYCH banks; and show how the NYCH suc-cessfully responded to the financial shock. In the second part we do the same for the banking disturbance in 1890. We provide estimates of the number of bank suspensions, describe the state of the money market in two contiguous periods – August to September and October to November – show how U.S. Treasury intervention by purchasing government securities forestalled a banking panic in August and September, and show how prompt action by the NYCH prevented a relatively mild banking unrest from escalating into a full-scale banking panic. The success of the New York Clearing House in forestalling at least two potentially serious banking panics has not been adequately appreciated.

Bank Suspension Estimates

We have reliable monthly estimates of bank suspensions from *Bradstreet's* (September 27, 1884, p. 197) during the 1884 panic. The estimates for the panic month of May by type of bank organization have already been given in the first chapter. Their significance is better grasped by comparing the panic month with the preceding and the following months (Table 3.1).

The number of national, state, and savings bank suspensions was strikingly small in the panic month – only sixteen. Sixty percent of the suspensions were brokerage houses whose demise was clearly related to the collapse of stock prices, seven of which failed in New York on a single day, May 14. The residue of bank closings in June was small. The Comptroller of the Currency (1884, p. xxxv) estimated that the liabilities of state and private bank closings in New York City exceeded $22 million and that the liabilities of the one national bank that failed in May were $4.5 million. There are no estimates for the interior. Deposits rather than liabilities are the preferred measure, but deposit estimates are not available.

A Narrative of the Banking Disturbance

A chronology of events during the month of May should pinpoint the sources of the banking disturbance in New York and reveal how fraud and imprudent management practices contributed to bank-specific unrest. Two such events occurred on May 6 and were the first of a series of shocks that undermined stability in the New York money market. Before noon the announcement was made of the failure of the Marine National Bank with deposits of $4.5 million at the time of closing, followed by the collapse of the brokerage firm of Grant and Ward. Former President U.S. Grant along with his son, Jim Fisk, and W. E. Smith were partners with Ferdinand Ward, an audacious speculator whose reputation for engaging in especially risky ventures was well known to Wall Street. Grant's name served as window dressing and added to the prestige of the house by enabling Ward to traffic on the reputation of his

Table 3.1. *Bank suspensions by type of bank organization, April–June 1884*

	National	State	Savings	Private	Total
April	2	1		6	9
May	5	7	4	26	42
June		2		10	12

Source: *Bradstreet's*, vol. 12, p. 197.

illustrious partner. Fisk, on the other hand, was also president of the Marine National Bank, which provided some of the funds to support Ward's speculative activities.

On the day the bank closed, there was indebtedness to the NYCH of $550,000, the result of a $767,000 overdraft by Grant and Ward. By permitting the overdraft, the bank apparently violated the law. When Marine National requested payment on Tuesday morning, payment was not forthcoming, and the bank was forced to close. Creditors eventually were paid 83.5 percent of their claims. Fisk was convicted in June 1885 and sentenced to ten years in prison. In October Ward also received a ten-year prison sentence.

The stock market remained calm in the face of the two failures. But not for long. On May 10, the Northwestern Car Co., of which Senator D. M. Sabin of Minnesota was the president and key owner, went into receivership; its demise was connected with the failure of Marine National. Stock prices which had begun to decline on Monday, May 12, turned into a "wildcat panic" on Wednesday.

But on that same day a startling revelation came to light. John Eno, president of Second National Bank, had embezzled $3 million and fled to Canada. A heavy run ensued all day on the 14th, amounting to at least $400,000. Fortunately, deposits in Second National were largely owned by New York residents without repercussions in the interior. Confidence in the bank was quickly restored when Eno's father made restitution for the stolen funds. Nevertheless, there had been a shock to confidence that reverberated throughout the credit markets.

The Metropolitan National Bank was also forced to close because of a serious run caused, according to the Comptroller of the Currency (1884, pp. xlii–xliii), by allegations that its president was speculating in railroad securities on funds borrowed from the bank and had loaned money to parties with similar interests. The Comptroller, however, could find no basis for such allegations. Rumor, not fact, accounted for depositor unrest.

The situation quickly deteriorated, creating panic on the stock exchange. Six brokerage houses failed which were either directly or indirectly connected with the president of Metropolitan National: Nelson Robinson, Goffe and Randle; Donald, Lawson and Simpson; Hatch and Foote; J. C. Williams and Hotchkiss; and Burton and Co. The Atlanta State Bank of Brooklyn failed; it was a correspondent of Metropolitan National. Two banks also closed which held balances with the Metropolitan: one in LaPorte, Indiana, and the other in Quincy, Massachusetts.

The *Commercial and Financial Chronicle* (May 16, 1884, p. 589) reported that "the wildest kind of panic raged, and securities were thrown overboard regardless of price." Call money was quoted as high as 4 percent for twenty-four hours. A contagion of fear that engulfed the stock market also extended to four banks within half a mile of the Exchange: Gallatin National Bank (deposits of $3.1 million), Phoenix National ($2 million), Union National ($3.8 million), and the Wall Street Bank (deposits unknown). However, none of the banks closed. Crowds of several thousand onlookers filled the sidewalks on Broadway from Pine Street to Exchange Place and from Wall Street to William Street (*New York Times*, May 14, 1884). There were also runs on five Brooklyn Savings Banks.

The closing of the Metropolitan Bank on May 14 was too important for the NYCH to ignore, especially because of its extensive relationships with interior banks. Two-thirds of its deposits ($7 million) were due to other banks; its closing could easily have spread fear and uncertainty throughout the country. To prevent that from happening, confidence needed to be restored. On the afternoon of the 14th the NYCH met and authorized the issue of loan certificates. But the action of the clearing house went beyond merely authorizing the issue of loan certificates. It intervened directly. After an initial consultation with the directors of the Metropolitan Bank, the NYCH appointed a committee to ascertain the bank's solvency. Upon learning that the bank had adequate safe securities for which certificates could be issued, the NYCH authorized the issue of $3 million of loan certificates to Metropolitan, part of which would be used to discharge immediately its indebtedness to the Clearing House. The bank reopened the next day, May 15, but chose voluntary liquidation six months later on November 18.

The NYCH issued over $24 million of loan certificates, $7 million of which were issued to the Metropolitan Bank. Only twenty of the eighty-two NYCH banks took out loan certificates. The largest amount outstanding at any one time was $21.9 million on May 24. The loan certificates had all been canceled by July 1 except those issued to the Metropolitan Bank, whose deposits had fallen from $11.3 million on May 15 to $1.3 million on September 30! The NYCH banks were willing to carry the loan certificates of the bank which on October 3 still amounted to over $5 million. The amount of loan certificates issued in 1884 compared favorably with the amount issued during the 1873 panic. Issues in 1873 amounted to $26.6 million against $21.9 million in 1884.

As a result of the stock market crash as well as the banking difficulties, the oil market also collapsed. Two banks failed in the oil region of Pennsylvania, the center of which was Bradford: Tuna Valley and the Exchange Bank. The Tuna Valley Bank held correspondent balances with the Metropolitan National. Runs followed on three other banks in Bradford. The Penn Bank of Pittsburgh, one of the larger Pittsburgh banks with deposits of $2.4 million, after undergoing a run for several days closed on May 21. There were runs on two other Pittsburgh banks. The Philadelphia Clearing House announced its willingness to support the Penn Bank, and it reopened two days later only to close again permanently on the 26th. Two banks in Boston also failed on the 15th.

On Thursday two more brokerage houses failed in New York: A. W. Dimock, and Fitch and Hatch. Because of its connection with Fisk and Hatch the Newark Savings Bank with deposits of $6 million closed. Fisk and Hatch owed the Newark Savings Bank over $1 million. Runs followed on two other savings banks in Newark: the Howard and the Dime savings banks. No other Newark banks were affected.

The Erie County Savings Bank (Erie, Pennsylvania) with deposits of $350,000 failed on May 19, causing "slight runs" on two other savings banks. There were also heavy runs on the banks in Petersburg, Virginia.

Another, this time minor, defalcation occurred on Saturday, the 24th, which forced the closing of the West Side Bank in New York City. A teller of the bank had fled to Canada after embezzling $85,000. The bank, however, was solvent and reopened on the last day of the month. No Treasury assistance was requested and none received during the 1884 panic.

What can we conclude from the brief narrative of the banking troubles in May 1884? There was no general loss of depositor confidence in either New York or the interior. The banking unrest was essentially local in nature with the possible exception of the closing of the Metropolitan National Bank, which was directly or indirectly responsible for at least four, if not more, bank failures: Atlanta State Bank of Brooklyn, Tuna Valley Bank of Bradford, Pennsylvania, City Executive Bank of LaPorte, Indiana, and Union Bank of Quincy, Illinois, and two brokerage houses:

Donald, Lawson and Simpson had $2 million locked up in the Metropolitan, and the sons of the president of Metropolitan were connected within Nelson, Robinson and Co.

There were only four bank closings excluding brokerage houses in New York including Brooklyn during the three-week crisis. And all four were related to the discovery of fraud and mismanagement, real or alleged, by the top officers of the banks. There were also runs on four banks contiguous to Wall Street and five Brooklyn savings banks, none of which was forced to close.

Bank closings in the interior were few, but that is not to say that the interior escaped entirely the effects of the unrest in New York. Interior banks withdrew balances from New York. But the withdrawals were minimal and did not lead to a suspension of cash payments as in 1873. The fact that cash payment was not suspended is a tribute to the speed with which the NYCH responded by providing assistance to the Metropolitan Bank, enabling it to reopen. There were runs on specific banks in at least six cities: New York; Brooklyn; Newark; Erie; Bradford, Pennsylvania; and Petersburg, Virginia.

The absence of any sizable or notable bank suspensions in the interior must not be interpreted to mean that banks outside New York did not respond to the banking disturbance in the central money market. For indeed they did, by withdrawing their New York balances. The weekly statement of the NYCH banks shows that the clearing house banks lost $19 million of reserves during the two panic weeks ending May 10 and May 14 (Table 3.2). The precarious state of the reserve position is revealed by the reserve deficit of $6.6 million for the week ending May 24. Had the reserve deficit persisted, loan and deposit contraction would have been more severe. Fear and uncertainty had spread to some interior banks though not to their depositors, and they responded by attempting to strengthen their reserve position. Total bank reserves had fallen almost 22 percent between May 10 and 24, but it did not pose a serious threat to the continuation of cash payments.

Was There a Banking Panic?

Unquestionably there was a panic in the classic sense in the stock market, attended by sharp price decreases in stocks and the closing of over ten brokerage houses. Call money could not be had except at exorbitant rates and large quantities of securities were unloaded on the market; there clearly was a crisis in the money and the credit markets deserving of the label of panic. But we may very well ask: Was there a banking panic? If we take the Calomiris-Gorton (1991, p. 112)

Table 3.2. *Changes in loans, deposits, and reserves during the first seven weeks of the 1884 panic and the amount of surplus reserves (first week, May 3–10) (in millions of dollars)*

	Change in loans	Change in deposits	Change in reserves	Change in surplus reserves
1st	−9	−3	+3	0.8
2nd	−6	−13	−5	4.4
3rd	−14	−20	−14	−6.6
4th	−3	−5	+2	−1.9
5th	−7	−5	+2	+1.34
6th	−7	−2	+6	+7.0
7th	−6	0	+2	+10.0

Source: Commercial and Financial Chronicle, vol. 38 (1884).

description of a panic: "Typically, all banks in a single geographical location are 'run' at the same time, and 'runs' subsequently occur in other locations," then there was no banking panic in 1884. The loss of depositor confidence was bank-specific, the exception being the runs on the four Wall Street banks, the five Brooklyn Savings banks, and the Petersburg, Virginia, and Bradford, Pennsylvania, banks. But with the exception of the last two cities, in no case did the runs extend to all banks in a single geographical location if geographical location refers specifically to city-wide suspensions.

A more precise description of what happened in 1884 is that an *incipient* panic was forestalled by the prompt and effective action of the NYCH. The issue of loan certificates especially to the Metropolitan Bank put out the fire in New York and thereby prevented its spread to the interior, as evidenced by the continuation of cash payments.

The Banking Disturbance of 1890

In the annals of banking panics, the 1890 episode, like that of 1884, is deserving of special consideration because of the evidence it provides of how a prompt response by the NYCH could forestall a general loss of depositor confidence before any serious damage could be done. The number of bank failures in both New York and the interior was small, even smaller than in 1884, and the economic effects minimal. The Comptroller of the Currency in his *Annual Report* for 1890 (p. 91) referred to events in November as the "Monetary Stringency of 1890." The phrase stuck and was repeated by Sprague (1910, p. 124) in his chapter describing what happened in 1890. However, his use of terms was not very discriminating. The label "crisis" was used for chapter headings in 1873, 1893, and 1907, and "panic" for 1884. He did not distinguish between crises and panics. But it is clear that Sprague recognized the special characteristics of the disturbance in 1890, though he did not emphasize its resemblances to 1884.

The comptroller and Sprague identified financial stringency as a money market state where there was a sharp curtailment of credit availability, especially to the stock market, and a spike in call money rates sometimes, not always, in conjunction with a reserve deficit of the NYCH banks. To relieve the reserve deficit, the NYCH banks responded by contracting loans, mainly call loans to the stock market, and thereby reducing deposits. Sprague attributed the custom to the reluctance of the NYCH banks to allow their reserves to fall below the required 25 percent minimum because of either a failure to understand or an unwillingness to act as though reserves were a resource to be used in emergencies rather than to be conserved.

Events in November 1890 reflected implicit panic-like characteristics which in the absence of NYCH intervention might have blossomed into a full-scale banking panic. The speedy authorization to issue loan certificates forestalled the spread of the disturbance from New York to the interior. In this instance as well as in 1884, action of the NYCH was sufficient to prevent a serious banking panic.

We know almost nothing about the incidence of bank closings in the interior during the 1890 episode. Neither the *Commercial and Financial Chronicle* nor *Bradstreet's* identified failures. However, *Bradstreet's* contains estimates of total business failures of all types including banks with liabilities in excess of $100,000 for November and December 1890. There were only fourteen failures of all types in the peak panic month of November, and fifty-four in December. We do not know how many of those failures were banks. But even if all fourteen were commercial banks, though that is highly improbable, that would still be a very small number indeed for an alleged peak panic month.

The number of bank suspensions in the two months can be narrowed further by *Bradstreet's* annual estimates of business failures for the year 1890, of which there were 194. Thirty-two of the 194 were private and state banks with $19 million of aggregate liabilities. Granted that the incidence of bank closings was greater in November and December, it is highly unlikely that all thirty-two occurred in the final two months of the year. Even if they did, the number of such failures in November

Table 3.3. *Bank suspensions by bank classification, November 1890*

	National	State	Savings	Private	Total
New York		1		9	10
Interior	1	2	1	4	8

Source: Authors[1] estimates.

and December would still reflect the mildness of the 1890 banking disturbance.

My estimates (Table 3.3) differ from those of *Bradstreet's*, which gives the total closures for the month as fourteen. The largest number of bank failures were brokerage firms: nine in New York, two in Philadelphia, and two in Richmond. The paucity of bank suspensions confirms the absence of any general banking panic in New York or the interior.

The banking disturbance in November was the culmination of stringent conditions in the money market that had begun in late summer and was postponed by heavy bond purchases by the U.S. Treasury. The decline in stock prices between May and October was greater than during the disturbance in November, though the decline was not so precipitous.

Beginning at midyear the foreign demand for American securities ceased. The sale of American securities in Europe began shortly thereafter. Years of British investment in South America, especially Argentina, were being terminated because of the difficulties that the Argentineans were having in making interest payments. London houses that carried a surfeit of unsold securities were forced to dispose of good securities to carry the load of the not-so-good. The repatriation of American securities caused the exchange rate to turn against the United States. Between mid-June and the second week in August, $15 million of gold was exported, one-seventh of the stock of New York reserves. Reserves in August were less than in June, a precarious state considering that the crop moving season had just begun.

Sprague identified two contiguous episodes of monetary stringency in 1890: The first extended from the third week of August through the second week in September, and the second commenced the week ending October 18 and ended the last week of November, culminating in a small number of bank closures. Tables 3.4 and 3.5 show the behavior of loans and surplus reserves of NYCH banks in each separate episode.

The data reveal that loan contraction at the NYCH banks was about equal in magnitude: $21 million between October 18 and November 29

Table 3.4. *Behavior of loans and surplus reserves of NYCH banks, August–September 1890*

	Loans	Surplus reserves
August 2	1.6	9.0
9	6.0	1.3
16	4.0	−0.7
23	−4.5	−2.5
30	−5.2	−0.5
September 6	2.5	−1.4
13	−1.8	−3.3
20	−0.6	1.9
27	1.4	1.4

Table 3.5. *Behavior of loans and surplus reserves of NYCH banks, October–November 1890*

	Loans	Surplus reserves
October 4	7.8	11.5
11	5.0	3.2
18	−0.7	−0.3
25	−4.0	−0.1
November 1	−2.8	0.7
8	−0.9	−2.5
15	−5.6	−0.8
22	−0.6	0.1
29	−2.6	0.4

and $14 million between August 9 and September 20. The decline in total reserves was about the same. Surplus reserves were negative in five statement weeks in the earlier period and in four statement weeks in the latter, the reserve deficit being almost uniformly higher between August and September. In the peak disturbance weeks in September and October call money rates varied between 1/8 and 3/8 percent per day.

What is significant about the earlier episode is the precarious state of the money market and bank reserves at the beginning of the crop moving season, which did not bode well in the event of an unanticipated shock. Sprague (1910, p. 128) conjectured:

It is probable that nothing more than the usual monetary stringency would have occurred in the autumn of 1890 had the country been able to escape the collapse of the speculative movement in England which culminated with the Baring Brothers failure in November.

Why was the banking disturbance postponed until November? Massive intervention in the government securities market with substantial purchases by the U.S. Treasury was the main reason why there were no bank closings in August and September. Money market participants had come to expect U.S. Treasury support to relieve monetary stringency and were dismayed when such action was delayed. And the Secretary of the Treasury did not hesitate to acknowledge his responsibility. In his *Report for 1890* he stated: "The growing surplus and the prospective needs of the country made it desirable that steps be taken to obtain more free offerings of bonds to the Government." Debt payment considerations also played an important role. The terms of debt repayment were more favorable when bond holders were disposed to sell their securities to the Treasury, namely during periods of money market stringency. But treasury purchases of government securities were not always feasible; they depended on an accident of surplus government revenue which did not always correspond with the needs of the money market. A treasury surplus simply enhanced demands for support, and conditions were favorable in August and September for Treasury intervention.

As we have seen, surplus reserves were negative beginning the week ending August 16 and continued through September 13 (Table 3.4). During the second week of the five-week period of reserve deficits call money rates varied between 12 and 20 percent per annum. On August 21, call rates rose to one-half of 1 percent per day, or more than 180 percent on an annual basis. The crop moving season was under way, with no visible means of financial support. To fill the breech the Treasury announced on August 21 its willingness to redeem immediately $20 million of 4.5 percent bonds with payment of full interest to maturity. The decision to purchase another $20 million of the same issue was made ten days later on August 31. The Treasury continued to inject more funds in September by paying out $18 million in anticipation of a year's interest on 4 percent bonds and making an additional offer to purchase $16 million of the same bonds. The total amount advanced by the Treasury since August 21 was more than $75 million to alleviate money market stringency. Surplus reserves turned positive for the week ending September 20.

Sprague (1910, p. 141) concluded that an insufficient reserve in New York during the first half of the year was the inevitable cause of the disturbance in the summer and autumn months. Intervention by the

Treasury in August and September to meet the crop moving needs prevented the situation from deteriorating into a full-scale financial panic. There were no prospects for Treasury support during the second money market disturbance since the Treasury's balance had slipped below $10 million.

The second money market disturbance in November created mild banking unrest in New York but a far more serious crisis in the stock market. The so-called panic of 1890 was a stock market panic which was triggered by the failure on November 11 of the large and well-respected brokerage firm of Decker, Howell and Co. with liabilities of $10 million. Antecedent conditions had made the market especially vulnerable. During the preceding statement week the NYCH banks had a reserve deficit of $2.5 million which contributed to the financial stringency by banks' contracting call loans. Call money rates were intermittently quoted between 1/8 and 1/2 percent per day. The failure of Decker, Howell and Co. unnerved the market, and stock prices collapsed.

The failure of the brokerage firm was attributed to its large holdings of the securities of the North America Company, formerly Oregon Transcontinental, identified with the Villard interests. When the price of North American stock fell from 31.5 to 17.5, Decker, Howell and Co. was in serious trouble, for it was unable to sell securities except at ruinous prices. As a result, Decker, Howell and Co.'s banker, the Bank of North America, was faced with a $900,000 shortage at the NYCH. It was the threat of the imminent collapse of the Bank of North America that prompted the NYCH to call an emergency meeting on the same day (November 11) for the explicit purpose of providing direct assistance to the bank and to Mechanics and Trader's Bank as well (deposits equal to $4.4 million) through the issue of loan certificates. The balance sheet statement for the Mechanics and Trader's Bank and the Bank of North America for three statement weeks is given in Table 3.6.

During the week of the banking disturbance the Mechanics and Trader's Bank was especially hard hit; it lost nearly $500,000 in deposits and half of its reserves. The Bank of North America lost almost 10 percent of its deposits. But what jeopardized the bank's solvency was the $900,000 shortage at the NYCH. Without assistance the bank had insufficient funds to cover the shortfall. Direct assistance had been provided on a previous occasion in 1884 to prevent the collapse of the Metropolitan National Bank. However, before the meeting of the Clearing House, nine large New York banks responding to the leadership of J. P. Morgan each agreed to contribute $100,000 for the purpose of diffusing the disturbance.

On November 12, the North River Bank in New York closed with

Table 3.6. *Balance sheet statement estimates, 1890 (in thousands of dollars)*

	Mechanics and Trader's Bank			
	Loans	Specie	Legals	Deposits
November 1	2,870	160	805	3,607
8	2,937	119	598	3,505
15	2,587	102	372	3,008
Change November 8–15	−350	−17	−226	−497
Percent	11.9		49	−14
	Bank of North America			
November 1	4,522	508	370	4,596
8	4,674	411	288	4,579
15	4,670	321	384	4,364
Change November 8–15	−4	−90	+96	−215
Percent	—	—	—	−9.6

Source: Commercial and Financial Chronicle, vol. 51 (Nov. 8 and 15, 1890).

deposits of $2 million, but its closing was unconnected to events in the stock market. Nine brokerage houses in New York and two in Philadelphia failed, six of them succumbing between November 11 and 18.

The market received a second shock later in the week. The famous banking firm of Baring Brothers in Great Britain was facing serious difficulties connected with its Argentinean financial ventures. On November 15, there were large sales of American securities both here and abroad. During the first two hours of trading, 400,000 shares were thrown on the market, sending stock prices tumbling. *Bradstreet's* described the frantic activity as follows (1890, p. 752): "The market on Saturday was the most excited half holiday ever witnessed on Wall Street." Call loans soared as high as 186 percent per annum. A syndicate headed by the Bank of England came to the aid of Baring's. A $15 million fund was made available to liquidate the Argentinean security holdings without further compromising the firm's solvency.

On Monday and Tuesday of the following week, two more New York brokerage houses closed. By Wednesday, however, the worst was over.

Table 3.7. *Behavior of select balance sheet items of New York banks November 8–29, 1890*

	Loans	Specie	Legal tender	Deposits	Surplus reserves
November 8	399	75	21	392	−2.5
15	393	74	22	387	−0.8
22	387	73	22	382	+0.1
29	385	72	23	379	+0.4
Net change		−14	−3	+2	−13

Source: *Commercial and Financial Chronicle*, vol. 51 (1890).

The stock market turmoil subsided and there were no more failures. Table 3.7 supplements the information contained in Tables 3.4 and 3.5 by revealing, in addition to loans and surplus reserves, the behavior of each of the components of total reserves and deposits. The reserve deficit declined substantially in the second week and became positive thereafter, and most important, the total reserves of the NYCH banks remained virtually unchanged, indicating that whatever hoarding had occurred in the interior did not come at the expense of the reserves of the NYCH banks. There was no necessity for a suspension of cash payments as in 1873. The NYCH had done its job well. An incipient panic had been nipped in the bud.

Did the Two Incipient Banking Panics Have Significant Economic Effects?

Now we come to perhaps the most difficult question of all, that is, trying to discover what impact banking unrest had, if any. The fact that bank suspensions were highly localized in New York and small in number might seem to suggest that we should not expect important economic consequences. Mildness of the banking difficulties may not, however, necessarily imply mildness of impact.

What kind of effects do we have in mind? Bank suspensions, if large enough, may contract deposits and hence the money stock. The mechanism is quite simple: The loss of depositor confidence as revealed by a shift from deposits to currency increases the currency-deposit ratio, a determinant of the multiplier, and if there is no change in reserves, the money stock will decline. This is at least one channel by which banking panics can affect the economy. Ben Bernanke (1983) has suggested that there may be a second channel; there may be a decrease in credit availability manifest in the difficulty of obtaining new loans. The absence of monthly data on the behavior of the money stock prevents our pursuing the search for money stock effects. Monthly estimates of the money stock begin in May 1907. Unfavorable effects of banking panics on long-term interest rates is another channel through which output and employment could be affected.

At the macroeconomic level we are interested in the relationship between banking panics, output, and unemployment. But again there are grave deficiencies in data availability. There are no monthly or quarterly data on any of the various measures of output and employment. We have annual estimates for GNP both nominal and real in 1880–93 and annual estimates for unemployment beginning in 1890. Annual estimates may, of course, very well smooth the effects of shocks occurring within the year and thereby give a misleading account of what actually happened. Nevertheless, they may identify effects that persist in subsequent years. Until the appearance of Christine Romer's (1989) and Balke and Gordon's (1989) annual estimates of nominal and real GNP, we had only the vaguest notion of what was actually happening to real economic activity. Now at least we have specific estimates with which to relate the timing and effects of banking panics without prejudging whether the relationship was causal or not.

What I find most informative is the absence of any real output effects in either panic year (see Table 3.8). But the evidence is ambiguous about whether the growth rate of GNP increased or decreased in the panic year. Romer's estimates reveal that the growth rate increased in both 1884 and 1890; it decreased in the post-panic year 1885 and increased in 1891.

The Balke-Gordon estimates show a decreased growth rate in both 1884 and 1890 and a decrease in the post-panic year 1885 and an increase in 1891.

The evidence is clear that there was no output contraction in the panic years, but that is not at all surprising for 1890 since the peak panic month was November. Moreover, there is no disagreement that the growth rate of real GNP decreased in the post-panic year 1885, but there is conflicting evidence about what happened to the growth rate in 1891.

Unemployment percentages for 1890–1898 are shown in Table 3.9, using both the Lebergott and the Romer estimates. There are no continuous estimates before 1890. Although there was no output loss in 1890 and 1891, the unemployment percentage increased in 1891 but did not persist into 1892.

Table 3.8. *Real GNP and GNP deflator*

	Romer				Balke-Gordon			
	Real GNP	Percent change	Price*	Percent change	Real GNP	Percent change	Price*	Percent change
1880	140		8.17		137.6		8.03	
1881	143.6	2.6	8.27	1.2	142.5	3.6	7.99	−0.5
1882	149.3	4.0	8.14	−1.6	151.6	6.4	8.16	2.1
1883	152.1	1.9	7.73	−5.0	155.3	2.4	7.88	−3.4
1884*	155.7	2.4	7.26	−6.0	158.1	1.8	7.53	−4.4
1885	157.8	1.3	7.17	−1.2	159.3	0.8	7.35	−2.4
1886	164.4	4.2	7.24	−1.0	164.1	3.0	7.35	0
1887	169.5	3.1	7.35	1.5	171.5	4.5	7.35	0
1888	168.9	−0.4	7.4	0.7	170.7	−0.5	7.47	1.6
1889	175.0	3.6	7.4	0	181.3	6.2	7.48	0.1
1890*	183.0	4.6	7.26	−1.9	183.9	1.4	7.3	−2.4
1891	191.8	4.8	7.17	−1.2	189.9	3.3	7.3	0
1892	204.3	6.5	6.89	−3.9	198.8	4.7	7.21	−1.2
1893*	202.6	−0.8	7.04	2.2	198.7	−0.1	7.23	0.3

Source: Romer, 1989, p. 22; Balke and Gordon, 1989, p. 84.
*1982 dollars.

Table 3.9. *Unemployment percentages*

	Lebergott's estimate	Romer's estimate
1890	3.97	3.97
1891	5.42	4.77
1892	3.04	3.72
1893	11.68	8.09
1894	18.41	12.33
1895	13.7	11.11
1896	14.45	11.96
1897	14.54	12.43
1898	12.35	11.62
1899	6.54	8.66

Source: Romer, 1986, p. 31.

There is another channel through which financial panics may adversely affect economic activity, and that is through a sharp and persistent decline in stock prices brought about through a stock exchange panic. How serious was the decline in stock prices in 1884 and 1890? The Cowles index of stock prices declined by 8.5 percent in May 1884 and 7.2 percent in November 1890. By comparison, the index declined by 10 percent in October 1929 and 33 percent between September and October. What happened in 1929 was not repeated in 1884 and 1890. In 1884 stock prices did not continue to fall, but they did not regain their April 1884 high until November of the following year. It was September of 1891 before the stock price index reached its October 1890 high. How much of a negative effect the 7 to 8 percent decline in stock prices may have had on expenditures cannot be properly assessed at this time.

The main characteristics of the decade of the 1890s were continuous price deflation and positive rates of economic growth. The GNP deflators employed by Romer and Balke-Gordon declined almost continuously from 1880 to 1891, a decrease of 12 percent in the Romer index and 9 percent in the Balke-Gordon index. Both indices show a one percentage point decrease in stock values in 1884 and 1.9 to 2.4 percentage point decrease in 1890.

Brief Review of Findings

The money market disturbances in 1884 and 1890 do not qualify as full-scale banking panics, for at least one key element was absent: There was no general loss of depositor confidence in either New York or the interior. The number of bank runs and bank closures was small, without significance for the country as a whole. There were nevertheless a panic in the stock market, sharp spikes in call money rates, and the abrupt curtailment in loan availability.

The credit for preventing a banking panic belongs to the NYCH in 1884, and to the NYCH and a J. P. Morgan syndicate in 1890. The NYCH intervened directly in 1884 to prevent the collapse of the Metropolitan National Bank; it appointed a committee to determine the bank's solvency. When the bank was judged to be solvent, the NYCH authorized the issue of $3 million of loan certificates immediately to Metropolitan, thereby forestalling the spread of the panic. The threat of the demise of the Bank of North America and Mechanics and Trader's Bank led the Clearing House in 1890 to provide direct assistance in the form of loan certificates. Furthermore, nine large New York banks under the leadership of J. P. Morgan agreed to contribute $100,000 each to the troubled banks. This is the first time that we hear of the presence of J. P. Morgan and his role in diffusing a financial crisis. In neither disturbance was there a perceived need by the NYCH to suspend cash payment. There has not been ample recognition that the NYCH behaved appropriately in thereby preventing two major banking panics. Its success lay in providing direct assistance immediately to the troubled banks; it did not rely on the initiative of the problem banks.

4 The Banking Panic of 1893

The banking panic of 1893 was unique among pre–World War I financial disturbances: Its origin was in the interior, primarily in the transappalachian West rather than New York City. It therefore bears a closer resemblance to the banking panics of the Great Depression than it does to the banking disturbances of 1873, 1884, 1890, and 1907, whose origin was New York City. Moreover, the central money market banks were less responsive to disturbances originating in the interior than they had been to shocks originating in the central money market itself, just as the Federal Reserve during the Great Depression had been less responsive to bank failures in the interior than it had been to disturbances in the New York money market. For that reason alone the 1893 panic warrants serious reconsideration.

But there is even a more compelling reason for revisiting the 1893 panic, namely, the existence of an unexploited data source of all bank suspensions for the period from January to September 1893. *Bradstreet's* listed all individual bank suspensions by seven geographical regions and five bank classifications: national, state, private, saving, and loan and investment companies. Given were not only closure dates but also dates when and if the closed banks resumed normal operations. Estimates were given of total assets and liabilities of each bank presumably at the time of suspension, but there were no separate estimates for deposits. The listing included 503 banks that suspended between May and August 1893 with liabilities totaling nearly $150 million, which represented approximately 8 percent of all banks and 2 percent of total bank liabilities. One-third of the suspended banks were probably solvent at the time of closure, and at least one in five resumed normal operations by September.

The *Bradstreet's* data enable us to construct for the first time estimates of the number of bank suspensions monthly and the liabilities of suspended banks January–August 1893. We are also able to show the incidence of bank suspensions by region and bank classification. We therefore have a basis for constructing an account of what happened during the 1893 panic that is more detailed than any of the other pre-1914 banking panics.

From the *Bradstreet's* data as well as from various newspaper sources we were able to identify five large cities – six if we count Kansas City, Missouri, and Kansas City, Kansas, separately – where the incidence of the panic was the greatest. Moreover, we were able to estimate both deposits (using newspaper data) and liabilities of suspended banks as well as the proportions of deposits and liabilities of closed banks that resumed operations by the end of October. The early resumption of normal operations of suspended banks is interpreted to mean that the banks were probably solvent at the time of closure. This may not have been true in every case, however. An average of over 40 percent of the banks in these six cities were solvent at the time of suspension, holding approximately half of the deposits of failed banks. The percentage of liabilities of failed banks that resumed was 88 for Louisville, 67 for Kansas City, and 50 for Portland and Denver. In these four cities depositors apparently made no effort to discriminate between solvent and insolvent banks at the time bank runs were under way. These estimates also represent one of the first attempts to quantify the extent to which frightened depositors exhibited their loss of confidence in both solvent and insolvent banks during bank runs.

The 1893 panic was special in other important ways as well. Unlike the 1873 panic, the New York Clearing House Association authorized in June the use of Clearing House certificates but did not partially suspend cash payments until August, almost six weeks later. The equalization of reserves as implemented during the 1873 panic might have prevented partial suspension in 1893. However, New York bankers were less willing in 1893 than they had been in 1873 to relinquish individual bank discretion over cash reserves for the purpose of shoring up weaker interior banks. Rather than accept an increase in the risk of losing reserves, they were prepared to tolerate a banking panic in the interior!

One of the keys to understanding banking panics is the behavior of currency held by the public. Depositor unrest is usually signaled by an abrupt increase in the public's holdings of currency – an increase in hoarding. Regrettably, there are no monthly estimates of either currency in circulation (currency held by the public plus vault cash in the banks) or currency in the hands of the public during the 1890s. Currency data include only the holdings of the banks: (1) specie and legal tender holdings of New York City banks weekly; (2) specie and legal tender holdings of central reserve city, reserve city, and country banks for all national banks at the four call dates: March 6, May 4, July 12, and October 3; and (3) annual data for all banks. Movements of currency between New York and the interior need not, however, have reflected increased hoarding by the public. Rather it may have signaled a desired increase by interior banks for excess reserves in anticipation of future deposit withdrawals. An important and sometimes overlooked part of the mechanism explaining what happened during the 1893 panic was the drain of currency from reserve city and New York City banks to bolster the reserves of the country banks, not simply to satisfy the hoarding propensities of the public. As we see below, there is some evidence that during the July panic the withdrawal of correspondent balances in at least a few cities such as Louisville played a destabilizing role along with currency hoarding by the public.

The first section presents a profile of bank suspensions during the panic months of May through August. The second section describes the stock market collapse and banking unrest in May, which as we see did not initiate a banking panic in either New York or the interior. The third section shows how the character of banking unrest changed in June. There were runs on savings banks as well as commercial banks in select cities. The fourth section concentrates on the principal panic month of July and describes in full detail city-wide panics in Kansas City, Missouri; Kansas City, Kansas; Denver; Louisville; Milwaukee; and Portland, Oregon, and identifies both the banks that suspended and the banks that reopened. In August the panic entered a new phase, described in the fifth section; bank suspensions remained high, but the banks suspended cash payment. The final section provides a brief summary and conclusions.

Profile of Bank Suspensions During the Panic

The number of bank suspensions and liabilities of suspended banks monthly from January through August is shown in Table 4.1. Bank suspensions began to accelerate in May, reached a peak in July, and declined thereafter. The four months May to August are considered by convention to be panic months, although there is some question whether a panic condition existed in May. June and July exhibit the greater intensity of banking disturbances with approximately 70 percent of both bank closures and liabilities of failed banks. It is also clear that the suspension of cash payment at the beginning of August did not bring an end to bank suspensions. More than 100 banks closed in August with liabilities equal to $25 million, or 17 percent of total liabilities of closed banks between May and August. In no other pre-1914 banking panic were banking suspensions in the interior more numerous.

Table 4.1. *Number and total liabilities of suspended banks,*
January–August 1893

	Number of suspensions	Liabilities of suspended banks (millions of dollars)
January	7	1.65
February	5	1.95
March	8	3.34
April	13	4.38
May	57	18
June	126	34
July	219	73
August	101	25
total	536	161.32

Source: *Bradstreet's*, September 23, 1893, pp. 599–601.

Table 4.2. *Number and total liabilities of suspended banks by region,*
May–August 1893

	Number of suspended banks	Percent of total	Liabilities of suspended banks (millions of dollars)	Percent of total
New England	12	2	10	7
Middle	22	4	7	5
Western	188	37	45	30
Northwestern	137	27	42	28
Southern	67	13	17	11
Pacific	68	14	27	18
Territories	9	2	1	1
Total	503		149	

Source: *Bradstreet's*, September 23, 1893, pp. 599–601.

Table 4.2 shows the geographical incidence of the banking crisis
between May and August by both the number of bank suspensions and
liabilities of suspended banks. *Bradstreet's* divided the United States into
seven regions. The Western region included such states of the transappalachian West as Ohio, Indiana, Illinois, Kentucky, Michigan, Missouri,
Kansas, and West Virginia. Excluded were Iowa, Minnesota, Wisconsin,

Table 4.3. *Number and liabilities of suspended banks for various classification of banks, May–August 1893*

	Number of suspended banks	Percent of total	Liabilities of suspended banks (millions of dollars)	Percent of total
National	142	28	67	45
State	149	30	32	22
Savings	41	8	15	10
Private	157	31	18	12
Loan and trust	14	3	17	11
Total	503		149	

Source: *Bradstreet's*, September 23, 1893, pp. 599–601.

Nebraska, and North and South Dakota, which were classified separately as the Northwestern region. California, Oregon, Washington, and Idaho were designated the Pacific region. What we observe in Table 4.2 is the high concentration of bank suspensions and liabilities of suspended banks in the Western and Northwestern states, with two-thirds of the bank closings and 60 percent of the liabilities of failed banks. Fewer than one-third occurred in the South and Pacific states. New England and the Middle Atlantic states escaped virtually unscathed. Three-quarters of the liabilities of closed banks were in the three regions: Western, Northwestern, and Pacific.

We can round out our description of bank suspensions during the 1893 panic by setting out the distribution of bank suspensions and liabilities of suspended banks according to type of bank organization, that is, national, state, private, savings, and loan and trust companies. The striking feature of Table 4.3 is that the number of bank suspensions was about evenly divided among national, state, and private banks, each accounting for a little less than one-third of the total. Nevertheless, national banks accounted for 45 percent of the liabilities of closed banks; state and private banks together accounted for only one-third of the total. Little significance attaches to the number of suspensions by private banks even though they were more numerous than all of the others; the amount of liabilities of closed private banks, however, was only slightly more than 10 percent.

Bradstreet's listing of all individual bank suspensions includes dates of those banks that resumed normal operations. We have assumed that

Table 4.4. *Number and liabilities of suspended banks by region that resumed operations, May–August 1893*

	Number of suspended banks that resumed operation	Percent of total number of suspended banks	Liabilities of suspended banks that resumed (millions of dollars)	Percent of total that resumed
New England	1	8.30	0.14	1.40
Middle	3	14.0	1.93	27.6
Western	39	21.0	9.14	20.3
Northwestern	17	12.4	3.93	9.30
Southern	13	19.4	6.26	36.8
Pacific	23	33.8	8.90	33.0
Territories	4	44.4	0.35	35.3
Total	100		30.65	20.5

Source: *Bradstreet's*, September 23, 1893, pp. 599–601.

suspended banks that resumed in less than three months were probably solvent at the time of closure. This conjecture is also supported by *Bradstreet's* estimates of assets and liabilities at the time of closure of banks that resumed. Table 4.4 lists suspended banks that resumed by region as well as their total liabilities and as a percentage of the total. For the country as a whole, one in five suspended banks resumed normal operations, having liabilities equal to the same percentage. The proportion of banks that resumed and the proportion of liabilities of failed banks differed substantially by region. One-third of the suspended banks in the Pacific states resumed with one-third of the liabilities of suspended banks; the Southern states had the highest proportion of liabilities of failed banks that resumed. As we see below both proportions were large in Denver, Louisville, and Kansas City, all of which experienced city-wide banking runs.

A profile of bank suspensions during the 1893 banking panic reveals a banking disturbance in the interior of the country of dimensions comparable to the banking panics of the Great Depression. Some 503 banks failed with liabilities equal to $150 million. The bank closures were not spread evenly throughout the country; they were highly concentrated in what we call today the Midwest. They were, however, fairly equally distributed among national, state, and private banks. Although bank suspensions were not greater among national banks, liabilities of closed national banks made up almost half of the total liabilities of suspended banks. One of the defining characteristics of the 1893 panic is the proportion of suspended banks that resumed normal operations.

The Stock Market Collapse and Banking Unrest in May

Two events served to herald the 1893 panic: the Philadelphia and Reading Railroad went into receivership on February 26, and the Treasury's gold reserve slipped below the $100 million danger threshold on April 21. The failure of the Philadelphia and Reading Railroad affected the stock market in March and April (Sprague, 1910, p. 163) with industrials absorbing most of the impact. And the decline in the Treasury's gold reserve below $100 million for the first time since resumption imparted some uncertainty about the future of the gold standard, particularly about the Treasury's ability to convert treasury notes issued to purchase silver into gold (Lauck, 1907, p. 97). Sprague, however, thought its influence was slight; he maintained (1910, p. 169) that distrust in the solvency of the banks in the West and Southwest rather than gold standard considerations "was clearly the direct cause which brought about runs upon banks and the numerous failures and suspensions."

There was no legislative mandate prescribing the size of the Treasury's gold reserve which had been created to insure the conversion of U.S. greenbacks into gold after the resumption of specie payments. Nevertheless, according to Dewey (1968, p. 441), "by tradition public sentiment adopted $100,000,000 as the line of demarcation between safety and danger." The Silver Purchase Acts called for the redemption of treasury notes in either gold or silver coin at the discretion of the Secretary of the Treasury, but, as a matter of fact, they were convertible into gold on demand. Silver purchases added to the Treasury's gold liabilities and created anxiety about the Treasury's ability to maintain gold convertibility of the note issue. President Cleveland, who was inaugurated in March 1893, had campaigned on a platform that called for repeal of the Silver Purchase Acts.

The immediate cause for concern in financial markets on April 21 was not so much the fact that the gold reserve had fallen below the target threshold but Secretary of the Treasury Carlisle's ill-considered public response. He stated that it might be necessary to redeem treasury notes in silver rather than gold, which was interpreted to mean that if the gold reserve dropped below the $100 million mark, the Treasury would be forced to pay out silver. The unfavorable reaction of the stock market was prompt – a "sensational day" in the stock market as described in the

New York Times. Early in the day the call money rate went as high as 15 percent. In the afternoon President Cleveland issued a statement affirming that treasury notes would remain redeemable in gold, thereby putting an end to speculation to the contrary. Stock prices recovered, and the call money rate returned to normal.

The damage, nevertheless, had been done. Secretary Carlisle's initial response had injected additional uncertainty into a highly volatile atmosphere. And the question of what the Treasury intended to do to restore the gold reserve still remained high on the agenda of the President, the Secretary of the Treasury, and leading Eastern bankers during the next two weeks.

On April 25, there was a sharp and severe drop of sixteen points in the stock of the Toledo, Ann Arbor and North Michigan railroad and a ten-point drop in American tobacco. The market attached no particular significance to the behavior of either of these two stocks.

There is no evidence in either March or April of any run on the Treasury's gold reserve for the purpose of exchanging treasury notes for gold. The impact, if there was one, of the decline in the gold reserve below $100 million was felt first in the stock market, but the immediate effects vanished quickly.

The stock market collapsed on May 3. The *New York Times* described the disturbance as the "nearest approach" to a panic since 1884. The general index of all stock prices fell 8.8 percent between April and May 1893 and 8.5 percent during the corresponding panic period during 1884. The index, unfortunately, refers only to monthly movements; there are no indexes for either daily or weekly changes in stock prices. The magnitude of the decline in all stock prices was roughly the same in both episodes. However, a decomposition of the all stock price index by type of stock (industrials, railroads, utilities) reveals that the disturbance was more severe in industrials in 1893 and utilities in 1884. The prices of industrials declined 15.7 percent in 1893 and the price of utilities 12.3 percent in 1884. According to the *New York Times*, panic was the only word to describe what happened to the price of industrials on May 3 and 4, 1893. The most active stock was National Cordage, which had declined from 75 in February to $18^3/_4$ on May 4. There had been a nineteen-point drop on May 3 and 4. Banks began calling the loans to National Cordage, and the company went into receivership on May 4. Three brokerage firms who were speculating in National Cordage stock also suspended operations.

The price adjustment in the stock market preceded by a day the failure of National Cordage, but once the adjustment was under way National Cordage took the lead in the collapse of industrials. During the last thirty minutes that the exchange remained open, National Cordage lost one-third of its value.

Although the failure of National Cordage on May 4 has received the most attention as the proximate cause of the 1893 panic, the break in stock prices on May 3 deserves equal consideration. The behavior of the price of National Cordage stock contributed to the severity of the decline in industrials, thereby provoking the firm's bank creditors to call their loans leading to its demise on May 4. But it was the break on May 3 that was largely responsible for bursting the speculative bubble in National Cordage stock and for precipitating the 1893 panic.

The upheaval in the stock market did not, however, initiate a threat of bank suspensions in New York nor, as we show, did it initiate a banking panic in the interior. There were, nevertheless, banking difficulties concentrated mainly in the "Western" states of Illinois, Indiana, and Michigan. Without prior warning the Chemical National Bank of Chicago closed its doors on May 8 with $1.6 million of deposits. Its closing did not come as a surprise to Chicago bankers, for they thought the bank had not been competently managed; excessive loans had been made to the bank's directors and to some of the shareholders (James, 1938, vol. 1, p. 581). The Chicago Clearing House Committee unanimously rejected its request for support. Because of the close association with Chemical National, the Capital National Bank of Indianapolis followed it into liquidation on May 11 with deposits of $1.1 million.

The next day, May 12, the Columbia National Bank of Chicago failed with $1.5 million of deposits as a result of the rumors precipitated by Chemical National (Anderson, 1954, pp. 74–75). The Columbia National, unlike Chemical National, had few individual depositors; most of its deposits were deposits with other banks, and its collapse provided a catalyst for transmitting the disturbance to surrounding states. Columbia National was affiliated with the Dwiggings-Starbuck chain of banks, including twelve small banks in Indiana and Illinois. It also had correspondent relationships with at least thirty country banks. Five state and one private Indiana bank closed the same day. During the next week seven more Indiana banks closed. The *Chicago Tribune* described the suspensions as "an ugly blow to confidence throughout the whole western territory." But there is no evidence that the public's confidence in the banks had been adversely affected.

The National Bank of Deposit in New York City failed on May 23 with $950,000 of deposits. More than $300,000 had been withdrawn in the preceding three weeks. The run was attributed to its alleged relationship with Columbia National in Chicago.

Table 4.5 shows bank suspensions and liabilities of closed banks by

Table 4.5. *Bank suspensions and liabilities of closed banks by region for May 1893*

	National		State		Saving		Private		Loan & trust		Total	
	Number	Liabilities*	Number	Liabilities	Number	Liabilities	Number	Liabilities	Number	Liabilities	Number	Liabilities
New England									2	0.75	2	0.75
Middle	2	1.8					2	0.5			4	2.3
Western	3	4.1	8	0.6			21	1.22			32	5.9
Northwestern	1	0.1	3	0.76			4	0.134	1	6	9	6.99
Southern	3	0.64	4	0.42			2	0.12			9	1.18
Pacific			1	0.48							1	0.48
Territories												
Total	9	6.64	16	2.26			29	1.97	3	6.75	57	17.6

Source: Bradstreet's, September 23, 1893, pp. 599–601.
* All liabilities in millions of dollars.

region and bank classification for the month of May. The three national bank suspensions (two in Chicago and one in Indianapolis) and the thirteen suspensions in Indiana account for one-half of the suspensions of the Western region and nearly 80 percent of the liabilities of failed banks in the region. There clearly was no widespread loss of depositor confidence in the Western states. And $6 million of the $6.9 million liabilities of closed banks in the Northwestern region is accounted for by the failure of one loan and investment company. Together these two regions explain over 70 percent of total bank suspensions during the month of May and nearly three-quarters of the liabilities of closed banks.

We can conclude that the banking disturbances in May were mainly local in nature without effects on general depositor confidence. There was no banking panic in May! Nor is there any evidence that these bank suspensions in the Midwest resulted in a run down of currency reserves of the New York banks, as we might have expected if there had been a serious loss of depositor confidence. The events in May can best be described as a financial crisis with the stock market collapse at center stage. Bank suspensions were not panic related, and there was no general loss of depositor confidence. The suspended banks in May presumably collapsed under their own weight, bringing down their affiliated banks as well without any connection with general financial conditions in the country as a whole.

Bank failures in Chicago were isolated events without perceptible effects on other Chicago banks, and the out-of-state repercussions seem to have been confined to affiliated and correspondent banks of the Columbia National and Chemical National banks. Henry Clews, a respected New York financial journalist, had written in the *St. Louis Post-Despatch* on May 21 "there was no widespread panic in the land and no prospect or fear of any."

There were numerous statements in urban newspapers about unrest among country banks that were withdrawing balances from correspondent banks as a precautionary measure. However, there is no evidence that New York City banks were shipping legal tender currency to the interior. In fact, the specie reserves of the New York banks did not change in May, and legal tender currency actually increased $13.5 million between April 29 and May 27.

The Banking Panic in June

In June the character of banking unrest changed. Runs on banks began that engulfed the cities of Chicago, Omaha, Milwaukee, Los Angeles, San Diego, and Spokane. In Chicago, Omaha, Detroit, Cleveland, and Kansas

City depositor unrest was concentrated solely among the savings banks. In 1893 the vast majority of workingmen were paid monthly in cash and had not yet developed the habit of using a checking account as a primary means of payment, but they did use savings banks as a depository for their savings. The savings banks were especially vulnerable to the loss of depositor confidence since the average deposit balance was small, and the individual depositor was not a financial sophisticate. In Chicago, for example, some savings banks were identified with a specific immigrant population such as the Hibernia Savings Bank (Irish). In Milwaukee, Spokane, Los Angeles, and San Diego depositor unrest was confined to commercial banks.

During the first week of June there were city-wide runs in Milwaukee, Spokane, and Chicago. Unrest spread during the second week to Omaha and Detroit. Los Angeles and San Diego bore the brunt of bank suspensions in the third week. The Plankinton Bank of Milwaukee closed on June 1 with deposits of $2 million; it had survived a "hard run" on May 13, the proximate cause of which had been the failure of a large furniture manufacturer who had amassed a debt of over $200,000 to the bank. Since that time there had been continuous withdrawals by large depositors. The bank's closing triggered a run on other banks in the city as well as the state.

There were three weeks of relative calm in Chicago after the suspensions of Chemical National and Columbia National banks in early May. On June 3, there was a renewal of banking unrest. Herman Schaffner and Company, the largest commercial paper house in Chicago, was forced to close with deposits of $850,000. The private bank had allegedly used funds to invest heavily in street railway bonds. As a result of the stock market collapse in May, the bottom had dropped out of the market for such bonds. The head of the firm committed suicide by renting a boat and rowing out into Lake Michigan, never to return. Alarm spread immediately among small depositors in the Jewish community. There followed runs on every savings bank in Chicago. Long lines of frightened depositors appeared at all of the savings banks. June 5 was described as the most exciting day in Chicago's financial affairs in a decade. The savings banks continued to pay depositors with one notable exception: the Dime Savings Bank, which paid only a percentage of deposits and then invoked the thirty-day withdrawal notice rule. There were no savings bank suspensions in Chicago. They were all financially sound as evidenced by their ability to meet depositors' demands. An editorial in the *Chicago Tribune* on June 7 contained the estimate that 4,000 depositors withdrew $1 million in two days!

Four banks failed in Spokane, Washington, on June 5 and 6 following the closing of the Bank of Spokane Falls. There were runs on nearly every bank in the city, though the banks were generally thought to be solvent.

On June 7 there was a run on the East End Savings Bank in Cleveland, but immediate action by the Cleveland bankers led to the restriction of payment to depositors. Similar action was taken by the fourteen savings banks in Detroit on June 12 after a run on the People's Savings Bank. The same day the People's Guarantee Savings Bank of Kansas City, Missouri, failed. And the following day June 13 the Kansas City Safe Deposit and Savings Bank, the largest savings bank in Missouri, suffered a run. The bank responded by restricting deposit withdrawals to thirty days. However, no other banks experienced runs.

Omaha was the next city engulfed by a run on its savings banks. The McCague Savings Bank of Omaha closed on June 12 with deposits of $377,000, and a run followed the next day on all the savings banks in the city. The suspension of the American National Bank of Omaha on June 13 with liabilities of $674,000 was attributed to the McCague family's association with the bank. The local Clearing House refused a request of American National for aid. The other nine national banks in Omaha were unaffected by the unrest among the savings bank depositors.

Within eight days there had been runs on the savings banks of Chicago, Omaha, and runs on individual savings banks in Detroit, Cleveland, and Kansas City, Missouri. Restrictions on deposit withdrawals in Detroit, Cleveland, and Kansas City prevented a general run on all the savings banks.

The New York Clearing House on June 15 took the unusual step of authorizing the issue of Clearing House certificates even though there was no banking disturbance in New York. Legal tender reserves of the New York City banks stood at $42.2 million on June 17, and specie amounted to $68.2 million. The statement of the New York City banks showed a decrease in legal tender currency of $16.5 million between June 3 and 17. The New York money market had remained calm without any external signs of stress. Philadelphia and Boston followed the lead of New York in the issue of Clearing House certificates.

At the beginning of the third week of June there were unprecedented runs in several California cities including San Francisco, San Bernardino, Los Angeles, and San Diego. Banking troubles began in Riverside on June 14 with the failure of the Riverside Banking Company, with deposits of $641,558, and spread quickly to the aforementioned cities. On June 21 four banks suspended in Los Angeles with deposits amounting to $1.7 million, and three banks suspended in San Diego. A total of twenty-five banks shut their doors throughout the state. Indeed what was remarkable was that all but seven reopened within a few days! Of these seven, three were expected to resume business shortly, and four were destined to close permanently. Those remaining closed included: one Los Angeles bank, the City Bank with deposits of $194,822; one San Francisco bank, the Pacific Bank with deposits of $2.1 million; and one San Diego bank, the Consolidated National Bank (no statement available). The Report of the California Board of Bank Commissioners (July 1893, p. 1) concluded that "California had suffered but little from the bank suspensions," a conclusion made more plausible by the speed with which the banks were able to resume normal activity.

Currency shipments to the Pacific Coast were unofficially estimated around $5 million. The statement of the New York City banks showed a decline in specie reserves of $2.3 million and legal tender currency of $3.1 million between June 17 and 24. The Pacific Coast banks held a larger proportion of specie to legal tender currency than did the banks in the East and Midwest because the public preferred specie to paper currency.

The significance of the bank failures in the Pacific states in June is revealed in Table 4.6. Some 126 banks failed in the country as a whole with liabilities of $34 million. Of the 126, some 44, or 35 percent, were located in the Pacific states with deposits equal to $16 million, or 47 percent of the total. California alone accounted for nearly 60 percent of the suspensions in the Pacific states and one-third of the liabilities of failed banks. More remarkable is the fact that 80 percent of the suspended banks resumed normal operations by the third week of July.

The Banking Panic in July

Bank suspensions accelerated during the second week in July with the highest concentration of suspensions and liabilities of suspended banks in the Western states – nearly one-half of the bank closings and 40 percent of the liabilities of closed banks (Table 4.7). If we include the Northwestern states as well, the percentage of failed banks rises to 72 percent and the percentage of liabilities of failed banks to 68. Bank suspensions remained negligible in the New England and the Middle Atlantic states.

The distinctive characteristic of the July suspensions, however, was city-wide panics in Kansas City, Kansas; Kansas City, Missouri; Denver; Louisville; Milwaukee; and Portland, Oregon. The closures in Kansas City, Denver, and Louisville accounted for one in four suspensions in the Western states but nearly 70 percent of the liabilities of closed banks. The bank failures in Milwaukee accounted for half of the liabilities of failed banks in the Northwestern states, and bank suspensions in

Table 4.6. *Bank suspensions and liabilities of closed banks, June 1893, by region*

	National		State		Savings		Private		Local & investment trust		Total	
	Number	Liabilities*	Number	Liabilities	Number	Liabilities	Number	Liabilities	Number	Liabilities	Number	Liabilities
New England												
Middle			4	3.32	1	0.12	3	0.41			8	3.85
Western	3	0.82	8	0.87	3	0.66	18	3.96			32	6.31
Northwestern	4	0.92	9	2.69	5	0.73	10	0.77	2	0.85	30	5.96
Southern	1	0.35	2	0.695	3	0.46	4	0.135			10	1.64
Pacific	14	7.1	21	5.23	3	2.65	6	0.88			44	15.86
Territories	1	0.098	1	0.188							2	0.286
Total	23	9.3	45	12.99	15	4.62	41	6.155	2	0.85	126	33.9

Source: Bradstreet's, September 23, 1893, pp. 599–601.
* All liabilities in millions of dollars.

Table 4.7. *Bank suspensions and liabilities of closed banks, July 1893, by region*

	National		State		Saving		Private		Loan & trust		Total	
	Number	Liabilities*	Number	Liabilities	Number	Liabilities	Number	Liabilities	Number	Liabilities	Number	Liabilities
New England	2	0.781			3	1.15			3	7.413	8	9.34
Middle			1	0.22			3	0.15			4	0.37
Western	34	17.527	35	3.31	11	5.64	23	2.148	2	0.31	105	28.94
Northwestern	16	9	20	8.33	2	0.32	14	1.808	1	0.8	53	20.26
Southern	10	1.49	4	0.075			7	0.62	1	0.76	22	2.95
Pacific	10	5.3	4	1.6	3	2.69	3	0.09	1	0.29	21	9.97
Territories	4	0.62			1	0.25	1	0.1			6	0.97
Total	76	34.72	64	13.54	20	10.05	51	4.92	8	9.57	219	72.8

Source: Bradstreet's, September 23, 1893, pp. 599–601.
* All liabilities in millions of dollars.

Portland, Oregon, alone make up one-third of the suspensions of Pacific states' banks but 60 percent of suspended bank's liabilities. The key, therefore, to understanding what happened in July is to understand what happened in these six cities. We describe the events that constitute the banking panic in each of the above six cities.

Kansas City

On July 11, the Kansas City Missouri Safe Deposit and Savings Bank, the largest bank in Missouri, with liabilities equal to $2 million, closed. The bank had withstood successfully a run on June 12, but deposit withdrawals were restricted at the time to thirty days. It was no surprise, therefore, that depositors returned thirty days later to reclaim their deposits. Depositors withdrew $150,000 the day the bank closed. The closing caused a drain on all financial institutions in Kansas City, Missouri. On the 14th the National Bank of Kansas City, Missouri, with liabilities of $4 million and with 108 country bank affiliates closed, spreading distrust over an even wider area; it had appealed to the Clearing House for $40,000, but as soon as the information became known by telegraph, correspondents and depositors set about withdrawing deposits.

July 15 has been described as the most critical day in the banking history of Kansas City, Kansas. Runs were made on all the larger banks. The Northup Bank, the oldest bank in Kansas City, and the Franklin Savings Bank failed. The failure of Northup Bank was related to the failure of the National Bank of Kansas City the previous day. The president of Northup was also the president of the National Bank of Kansas City. Deposit withdrawals were heavy at every national bank in Kansas City. There were eight national banks with deposits totaling $11.8 million.

Two days later on July 17 the Missouri National Bank of Kansas City suspended with over $900,000 of deposits. One-half of the deposits were withdrawn within one week. The Bank of Grand Avenue and Citizen's Bank suspended the same day.

Listed in Table 4.8 are the Kansas City banks (both Missouri and Kansas), the dates of resumption, and amount of deposits and liabilities of failed banks. A total of eight banks in Kansas City, Kansas, and Kansas City, Missouri, failed over the course of a week with liabilities of over $7 million. However, nearly 70 percent of the liabilities were in four banks that resumed payment. We also have data on state bank suspensions in Kansas and the amount of deposits of suspended banks which we have rearranged on a weekly basis June through August (Table 4.9). The diffusion of the banking crisis throughout the state is revealed during the second and third weeks of July when nineteen state banks suspended

Table 4.8. *Failed Kansas City (Missouri and Kansas) banks, 1893*

	Date of suspension	Deposits ($)	Liabilities ($)	Date of resumption
Kansas City Safe Deposit Bank	July 11	N.A.*	2,000,000	
National Bank of Kansas City, Missouri	July 14	3,000,000	4,000,000	October 4
Northup Bank of Kansas City, Kansas	July 15	308,000	150,000	
Franklin Savings Bank, Kansas City, Kansas	July 17	N.A.	65,000	
Armourdale Bank, Kansas City, Kansas	July 17	N.A.	100,000	August 15
Missouri National Bank, Kansas City	July 17	900,763	700,000	July 31
Bank of Grand Avenue	July 17	N.A.	175,000	August 27
Savings Bank, Kansas City, Missouri	July 17	*N.A.*	*N.A.*	
Citizen's Bank	July 18	69,603	150,000	
Total		4,278,366	7,340,000	4,975,000

with deposits totaling nearly $1 million. Five national banks in Kansas outside Kansas City suspended between July 14 and 22 with deposits of $433,620. Four of the banks resumed operations in August and one in September. More than thirty banks including national banks failed in Kansas with deposit losses totaling $5.7 million at a minimum. Deposits in banks that resumed payment amounted to $4.3 million or 75 percent of the deposits of closed banks.

Denver

Beginning July 17 and continuing for three days there were runs on all the banks in Denver. Twelve banks were forced to suspend with deposits equal to at least $4.8 million and liabilities equal to $6.6 million. Of these twelve, six were national banks, five were savings banks, and one was a private bank. At least five of Denver's national banks were able to withstand the drain.

Table 4.9. *Kansas state bank suspensions, 1893*

	Number	Deposits in suspended banks ($)
June		
1st week	1	N.A.*
2nd week	2	82,105
3rd week	4	614,505
4th week	2	28,280
Total	9	724,890
July		
1st week	5	68,346
2nd week	3	69,357
3rd week	16	929,292
4th week	3	57,844
Total	27	1,066,995
August		
1st week	—	—
2nd week	—	—
3rd week	2	12,624
4th week	—	—
Total	2	12,624

Source: *Second Biannual Report of the Bank Commissioner of the State of Kansas*, September 1, 1894, Topeka, 1894.
*N.A.: Data not available.

There is no external shock that can be readily identified that will explain the run on the savings banks in Denver on July 17. Unrest among depositors at the Denver Savings Bank had begun at the end of May. On May 27 the Denver Clearing House Association had requested that the savings banks enforce the thirty-day rule for the withdrawal of deposits in response to the run on the People's Savings Bank. Savings bank depositors may simply have been responding to the termination of the thirty-day rule where it was in effect. Three savings banks and one national bank closed on July 17. The next day two national banks and three state and private banks suspended. On the morning of July 19 the panic was on in earnest. As one newspaper described it, there was a continuous mass of clamoring humanity stretched down all of the streets near Denver's banks. The State National, the German National, and

Table 4.10. *Failed Denver banks, July 1893*

	Date of suspension	Deposits ($)	Liabilities ($)	Date resumed
People's Savings Bank	July 17	1,300,000	1,125,000	
Rocky Mountain Dime and Savings Bank	July 17	50,000	105,000	
Colorado Savings Bank	July 17	435,109	642,000	
Union National Bank	July 17	321,000	1,300,000	August 21
National Bank of Commerce	July 18	753,992	850,000	August 17
Commercial National Bank	July 18	N.A.*	400,000	
Capital Bank	July 18	N.A.	N.A.	
North Denver Bank	July 18	N.A.	N.A.	
Mercantile Bank	July 18	N.A.	45,000	
State National Bank	July 19	550,891	635,000	August 29
German National Bank	July 19	1,173,587	1,143,000	August 29
People's National Bank	July 19	210,000	389,000	August 21
Total		4,794,579	6,634,000	4,317,000

*N.A.: Data not available.

People's National Bank closed. Deposit withdrawals in Denver since May 1 were estimated to be nearly $8 million, $3 million of which was sent to the East and $5 million of which was hoarded.

The Comptroller of the Currency attributed the runs on Denver banks to the loss of confidence of many small depositors and not to poor or fraudulent management practices. Support for the Comptroller's assessment comes from the fact that five out of six national banks, including the largest, resumed during the month of August holding roughly two-thirds of the deposits of failed banks. In Table 4.10 are given the names of the failed banks, estimates of deposits and liabilities, and when the banks resumed operations.

Louisville

Five large Louisville banks suspended operations between July 22 and July 25, with deposits totaling $1.7 million and liabilities of $4.5 million. This large discrepancy between deposits and total liabilities is obviously attributable to different reporting dates. The deposit data were extracted from local newspaper files, and total liabilities from *Bradstreet's*. Newspaper data were more likely to be nearest reporting date and *Bradstreet's* at the time of suspension.

When the Kentucky National Bank closed on July 22, there were no visible signs of panic at Kentucky National nor any other Louisville bank. The bank had lost more than $900,000 of deposits since May 1 and allegedly had been in difficulty for the past two and a half years. On July 23, the Louisville City National Bank failed with no run nor trace of depositor unrest. The immediate cause of suspension was a panic withdrawal of balances by correspondents rather than distressed depositors. The next day Merchant's National closed its doors for the same reason – withdrawal by out-of-town correspondents. Only then did small depositors begin to run on at least six other Louisville banks. The Louisville Deposit Bank and Fourth National failed, the first because of depositor withdrawals, the second because of immediate calls from its country correspondents. Finally on July 26 the Louisville Clearing House announced that assistance would be provided to banks in need of support. Why they waited so long is not known.

The four national banks that suspended temporarily were presumably solvent at the time of closure; three resumed normal operations in a little over a month, and one in two weeks. Deposits of banks that resumed constituted three-quarters of the deposits of failed banks and nearly 90 percent of total liabilities. The number of suspended banks, date of suspension, deposits and liabilities of failed banks, and dates of resumption are given in Table 4.11.

The Louisville experience was exceptional inasmuch as the suspension of at least three of the five banks can be attributed to "panic" withdrawals not by ordinary depositors but by out-of-town correspondent banks. Also the fact that four out of the five resumed operations within two months supports the view that depositors were indifferent among solvent and insolvent banks.

Milwaukee

Although there were only four suspensions in Milwaukee between July 22 and 29, the amounts of deposits and liabilities of failed banks were greater than any of the other six cities. Denver had the largest number of individual bank suspensions with twelve, but liabilities of failed banks was only $6.6 million compared with $9.7 million for Milwaukee. The largest bank to close during the July panic was the Marine and Fire Insurance Company Bank or the "Mitchell Bank," one of the more well-known private banks in the country with liabilities of $6

Table 4.11. *Failed Louisville banks, July 1893*

	Date of suspension	Deposits ($)	Liabilities ($)	Date of resumption
Kentucky National Bank	July 22	470,693	1,742,000	October 2
Louisville City National Bank	July 24	222,000	467,000	August 29
Merchant's National Bank	July 25	380,838	1,151,000	August 29
Louisville Deposit Bank		418,000	539,000	
Fourth National Bank		174,387	548,000	August 26
Total		1,665,918	4,447,000	3,908,918

million. Although two banks had suspended on July 22, the failure of the Mitchell Bank on the 25th shattered depositor confidence and caused a well-defined run on most of the other banks in the city. The size of the run on the bank is revealed by the bank's July 1 statement when deposits were listed as equal to $7 million and on the date of suspension $5.8 million, a sharp decline of $1.2 million in a little more than two weeks.

As we have seen above, there was a previous run on all the banks in Milwaukee on June 1 and 2 precipitated by the failure of the Plankinton Bank on June 1; the Plankinton Bank had survived a serious run on May 13. The seeds of depositor uncertainty and unrest had been sown on the earlier dates, but the ultimate collapse came in July. The names of the suspended banks and other relevant information appear in Table 4.12.

Portland, Oregon

During the last week in July seven Portland banks suspended with liabilities equal to $6 million (see Table 4.13). Four national banks were forced to close with one-half of the liabilities of the suspended banks but each resumed operations before the end of September. The largest of the bank failures was the Portland Savings Bank with liabilities of $2.5 million, but its failure was directly attributable to the collapse of the Commercial National Bank with which it shared the same management. The failures in Portland made up one-third of the bank closings in the Pacific states in July and 60 percent of the liabilities of suspended banks.

Table 4.12. *Milwaukee bank suspensions, July 1893*

	Date of suspension	Deposits ($)	Liabilities ($)	Date of resumption
Milwaukee National	July 22	413,857	1,300,000	September 25
South Side Saving		1,021,465	1,200,000	
Wisconsin Fire and Insurance	July 25	5,844,008	6,000,000	Jan. 15, 1894
Commercial Bank of Milwaukee	July 29	3,215,813	1,184,000	
Total		10,495,135	9,684,000	1,300,000

Table 4.13. *Portland, Oregon, bank suspensions, July 1893*

	Date of suspension	Deposits ($)	Liabilities ($)	Date of resumption
Oregon National Bank	July 27	365,108	650,000	September 9
Northwest Loan and Trust Co.		N.A.	600,000	
Union Bank Co. Savings Bank	July 28	N.A.	52,000	
Ainsworth National Bank	July 29	447,000	530,000	September 15
Commercial National Bank		455,000	1,500,000	September 26
Portland Savings Bank		N.A.	2,450,000	
East Portland National Bank		114,211	265,000	September 16
Total		1,381,319	6,047,000	2,945,000

Tables 4.14 and 4.15 summarize the data in the text for the six cities. Table 4.14 shows the number and deposits of suspended banks with dates of resumption and percentage of deposits and liabilities of banks that resumed operation. Table 4.15 classifies the suspended banks in the five cities; that is, whether they were national, state, private, savings, or

Table 4.14. *Six-city comparison of suspended and resumed banks, July 1893*

	Date of panic	Number of suspensions	Deposits in suspended bank ($)	Liabilities of suspended banks ($)	Number of resumptions	Perent	Deposits in resumed banks	Percent	Liabilities of resumed banks	Percent
Kansas City (Mo. & Ks.)	July 11–17	8	4,278,366	7,340,000	4	50	1,125,000	26	4,975,000	68
Denver	July 17–19	12	4,794,579	6,634,000	5	42	3,009,470	63	4,317,000	65
Louisville	July 22–25	5	1,665,918	4,447,000	4	80	1,247,918	74	3,908,000	88
Milwaukee	July 22–29	4	10,495,135	9,684,000	1	25	413,857	4	1,300,000	13
Portland	July 27–31	7	1,381,319	6,047,000	4	57	1,381,319	100	2,945,000	49
Total		36	22,615,317	34,152,000	18	50	7,177,564	32	17,445,000	51

Table 4.15. *Six-city comparison, national, private, and savings Banks, 1893*

	National banks			Private and state banks			Savings banks		
	Number	Deposits	Liabilities	Number	Deposits	Liabilities	Number	Deposits	Liabilities
Kansas City (Mo. & Ks.)	2	3,900,763	4,700,000	3	377,603	400,000	3	N.A.	2,650,000
Denver	6	3,009,470	4,717,000	3	N.A.	45,000	3	1,785,109	1,872,000
Louisville	4	1,247,918	3,908,000	1	418,000	539,000			
Milwaukee	1	413,857	1,300,000	2	9,059,821	7,184,000	1	1,021,465	1,300,000
Portland	4	1,381,319	2,945,000	1	N.A.	600,000	2	N.A.	2,502,000
Total	17	9,953,327	17,570,000	10	9,855,424	8,768,000	9	2,806,574	8,324,000

investment and loan companies, and the amount of deposits and liabilities in each classification.

Of the thirty-six suspensions in the six cities in July approximately one-half were national banks, one-quarter private and state banks, and one-quarter savings banks. National banks accounted for half of the liabilities of failed banks, and the other half were about equally divided between savings and private and state banks. Of the thirty-three national banks that failed between July 14 and August 1, half were in those six cities.

What is especially striking about Table 4.14 is the fact that half of the banks that failed resumed normal operations. The proportion varied by city, from a high of 80 percent for Louisville to a low of 25 percent for Milwaukee, excluding Wisconsin Fire and Insurance which did not reopen for six months. The banks that resumed accounted for 50 percent of the liabilities of failed banks. Again the ratio varied by city – above 65 percent in three of the six cities.

Partial Suspension, the Currency Premium, and the Gold Inflow

On August 3 the New York banks severely restricted, though they did not completely halt, the shipment of currency to the interior, and the Treasury's gold reserve fell below the $100 million threshold. The panic had entered a new phase. Although the number of bank suspensions remained high, it was the scarcity of currency that commanded the most attention. The August 5 statement of the New York Clearing House banks showed a reserve deficiency of $14 million. Specie reserves amounted to $56 million and "legals" to $23.3 million. Reserves remained well above the low points reached during the 1873 panic. In the earlier panic legal tender reserves had fallen as low as $5.8 million down from $34 million on September 20, 1873. In August 1893 New York banks were simply unwilling to suffer a further decline in their reserves. They gave as their reason the fact that further depletion might lead to a loss of depositor confidence – presumably in New York banks. Unlike in 1873 they balked at the suggestion of introducing a reserve equalization scheme to prevent the burden of reserve losses from falling too heavily on any one bank. Neither were they willing to adopt this policy in August 1893. Sprague (1910, p. 181) maintained that "the real reason for suspension was that which was pointed out in the report of the Clearing-House Committee in 1873. The drain had not fallen evenly upon the banks."

The proximate effects of suspension of cash payments were four: (1) A premium on currency emerged immediately and continued for thirty days (28 in 1873); (2) currency shipments continued to interior banks on a reduced scale – $5 million the first two weeks, $6 million the third week, and $2 million the fourth week for a total of $13 million (Sprague, 1910, p. 181). Between July 29 and August 29 legal tender currency of the New York banks declined by $6.4 million. (3) Bank suspensions continued at a reduced rate; and (4) the demand for currency by country banks became urgent.

The reluctance of New York to ship currency created a currency famine in the interior as reflected in the premium of currency in New York and other cities. New York exchange was quoted in Chicago at between $7 and $10 per thousand during the first week of August. On August 9 currency was selling at between $15 and $25 per thousand in Boston. The Clearing House banks in Richmond would not pay over $50 per bank customer. Banks in New Orleans refused to ship currency to pay cash against demand deposits. In Indianapolis drafts on New York banks from country correspondents were refused; they proudly announced that there was "plenty of money for patrons," but none for New York! The premium on currency remained high throughout most of August; by the 29th it had fallen to $3/4$ percent; thereafter, it vanished entirely.

There were at least several effects of the currency shortage, some negative, some positive. Friedman and Schwartz (1963, p. 110) have argued that the premium on currency reduced the utility of deposits relative to currency that increased the currency/deposit ratio quite apart from depositor distrust of the banks. The widespread refusal to honor drafts on New York had a dampening effect on the shipment of grain and other commodities to the East Coast. On the positive side the currency premium led to an exchange rate adjustment so that it became profitable to import gold, and the direct importation of gold not only at New York but also at Chicago as well ultimately relieved the currency shortage.

The partial suspension of cash payments did not eliminate bank suspensions, contrary to the conclusion of Friedman and Schwartz (1963, p. 110): "Restriction of cash payments brought to an end the stream of bank failures." Table 4.16 shows the number of bank suspensions, deposits, and liabilities of suspended banks by region and by bank classification. Some 101 banks closed their doors in August with liabilities of $25 million. A little less than one-half of the closures were located in the Northwest with liabilities equal to one-third of the total liabilities of failed banks. Suspensions were negligible in New England, Middle, and Pacific states.

During the first week in August there was a run on the savings banks in New York City. On August 1, the Seven Corners Bank of St. Paul,

Table 4.16. *Bank suspensions and liabilities of closed banks by region, August 1893*

	National		State		Saving		Private		Loan and trust		Total	
	Number	Liabilities (millions of dollars)	Number	Liabilities (millions of dollars)	Number	Liabilities (millions of dollars)	Number	Liabilities (millions of dollars)	Number	Liabilities (millions of dollars)	Number	Liabilities (millions of dollars)
New England			1	0.225			1				2	0.225
Middle	1	0.2	1	0.25			4	0.30			6	0.75
Western	6	1.09	5	1.3	1	0.035	7	0.54			19	2.97
Northwestern	15	6.76	11	0.99	3	0.19	16	1.22			45	9.16
Southern	12	8.02	5	0.753	2	0.09	7	1.95			26	10.81
Pacific							2	0.81			2	0.81
Territories	1		1	0.045							1	0.045
Total	34	16.07	24	3.56	6	0.315	37	4.82			101	24.77

Source: Bradstreet's, September 23, 1893, pp. 599–601.

Minnesota, failed with deposits amounting to $1 million. Three days later the National German American Bank with deposits of $2.6 million closed, followed by the suspension of the West Side Bank. And on August 9 a banking panic struck Nashville, Tennessee. The First National collapsed with deposits of $1 million. Runs followed on the American National Bank which failed on August 10 and the Fourth National. The City Savings Bank restricted payment by invoking the sixty-day rule. The 1st National Bank of Dubuque, Iowa, with deposits of $520,000 suspended due mainly to the withdrawals of balance of country bankers. None of the remaining banks faced a run. The spate of urban banking panics may have decelerated in August, but bank suspensions continued at a reduced rate.

The onset of the near panic in the stock market in early May did not cause a banking panic, though the number of bank suspensions increased. A serious financial disturbance, however, was in the offing. Nor did it initiate an economic contraction. The decline in economic activity had been under way since January; the National Bureau of Economic Research identified a cyclical peak in January 1893 and a trough in June 1894. Hoffman (1970, p. 55) without the benefit of GNP estimates thought that the contraction had begun in January with a decline in the prices of wheat and iron accompanied by falling prices in the stock market, a contra seasonal flow of money to the interior and a dwindling trade balance. Moreover, the retardation in economic activity had been noted in all of the contemporary business journals.

Contractionary forces accelerated in August with the partial suspension of cash payments. Sprague (1910, p. 100) conjectured that suspension accentuated the decline in output by (1) increasing the general feeling of distrust, (2) making it more difficult to get cash for payrolls, and (3) deranging the exchange between different sections of the country and delaying the movement of commodities. His evidence consisted of showing that railway earnings had fallen twice as much in August as in July; Clearing House transactions decreased 30 percent in August compared with 15 percent in July; and factories temporarily closed because of an inability to obtain cash for payrolls.

The unsettled situation in August, unlike banking panics in the South and West in July, was manifest in all sections of the country. Hoarding increased, but there are no data on currency in circulation in the interior to confirm or deny this inference. The suspension of cash payments generated economic trauma, leaving a residue of distressing experiences which etched itself in the public's mind.

Public sentiment and selective indicators of business activity can easily exaggerate what happened to aggregate output and employment. Christine Romer's (1989, p. 22) and Balke and Gordon's (1989, p. 84) new estimates of annual real GNP and Hoffman's (1970, p. 109) estimate of unemployment during the winter of 1893 and 1894 provide the basis for estimating the impact of the banking panic. Unfortunately, the data on output and unemployment tell contradictory stories. Since the downturn began in January and continued through the remainder of the year, we can use Romer's and Balke and Gordon's estimates of real GNP for 1893 to discern what happened to output. Romer found that real GNP declined by only 0.8 percent in 1893 and 0.9 percent in 1894. Balke and Gordon's estimates showed no change in 1893 and a 2.9 percent decline in 1894. If these estimates are reliable, the contraction in 1893 and 1894 was less serious than contemporary and subsequent accounts would have us believe. Both estimates convert an economic depression into a relatively mild recession.

Hoffman (1970, p. 109) estimated the unemployment percentage for the winter of 1893–94 to be between 17 and 19 percent. But these harsh estimates are difficult to reconcile with Romer's and Balke and Gordon's real GNP estimates for both years. Both sets of estimates are subject to wide margins of error. Nevertheless, the paradox remains unresolved, that is, how such a mild decline in real GNP was associated with a substantial unemployment percentage.

Summary and Conclusions

In this chapter, I have attempted to fill a lacuna in our knowledge of the panic of 1893. Sprague (1910) clearly recognized that the banking crisis was a result of banking operations in other parts of the country. Furthermore, he acknowledged that the situation differed from all previous banking panics under the National Banking System inasmuch as there was widespread distrust of the banks in the interior, mainly in the South and West. However, he merely mentions but does not describe the bank suspensions in Denver, Chicago, Indianapolis, Milwaukee, and Louisville. His primary concern was what was happening in the New York money market and the reaction of the New York City banks. We fill that gap in our knowledge by reconstructing the events in the interior that constitute the 1893 panic.

The most surprising conclusion to emerge from the narrative of what happened in the six cities during the July panic is the proportion of banks that suspended and resumed operations within three months. We regard those banks as solvent at the time of closure. It is indeed striking that over 90 percent of the banks in Kansas City and Portland and 65 percent in Louisville and Denver were solvent at the time of the bank runs. We simply have not been able to estimate the proportion of solvent to insolvent banks during any of the banking panics in U.S. history. This study is a step in the right direction.

It is also of great interest to have learned that the response of the New York banks was asymmetric, that is, their response to banking suspensions in the interior was not as vigorous as their response to panics that originated in the New York money market in 1873. In this respect the 1893 panic bears a strong resemblance to the Fed's weak response to bank suspensions in the interior during the Great Depression, and its strong response to disturbances in the New York money market. The central money market held center stage in both panic episodes. Events on the periphery were secondary.

What has also emerged from our study is the destabilizing role of the country banks whose panic-like behavior led to the withdrawal of bankers' balances when there was no actual threat of runs by depositors. The withdrawal of balances from New York went to satisfy not only depositors' demands but also the increased demands of country banks. We have shown how the withdrawal of correspondent balances led in some instances to bank suspensions, especially in Louisville and in banks in other cities as well.

We have also shown that the partial suspension of cash payment did not, contrary to the views of Friedman and Schwartz, eliminate bank suspensions.

5   The Trust Company Panic of 1907

Fourteen years had elapsed since the last serious banking disturbance in 1893. No attempt had been made in the interim to devise a strategy for preventing banking panics. The association of NYCH banks was still a loose alliance of fifty-two member banks with deposits totaling more than $1 billion. Thirty-three banks including state banks and trust companies remained outside with deposits of almost $800 million. Although prepared to act in the interest of all NYCH banks, the NYCH was not disposed to offer direct financial support to nonmembers even if withholding support increased the risk of failure to themselves. Its responsibility for preventing banking panics, well understood before 1873, had by now been mostly forgotten. The absence of strong leadership gave dissident voices in the Clearing House the opportunity to express purely self-serving interests at the expense of those who had a clear understanding of the broader role of the association of New York banks.

Three characteristics of the 1907 panic render it unique among the banking panics of the national banking era: (1) the disturbance in New York was largely confined to the trust companies; (2) leadership for restoring banking stability was assumed by J. P. Morgan and not the New York Clearing House; and (3) the instrument of voluntary money pooling was used extensively to provide financial support to troubled trust companies and the stock market, and to relieve the fiscal crisis in New York City.

A trust company-specific banking panic created problems not encountered in earlier panics. Trust companies were not members of the NYCH, though the Knickerbocker Trust did clear through a member agent; moreover, they had no trade association nor any other formal or informal organization to which they could appeal for financial support in time of crisis. And the NYCH felt no responsibility to come to their aid. Intense rivalry between the member banks and the trust companies for

83

deposits tended to obscure the fact that the loss of depositor confidence might strike the trust companies as well.

The unwillingness of the NYCH to intervene to save the Knickerbocker Trust created a leadership vacuum which was promptly filled by J. P. Morgan, who upon returning to New York on October 19 attempted to organize the trust company presidents for the specific purpose of coming to the aid of the troubled banks. Morgan's bank was not a member of NYCH though he attended by invitation the meeting of the NYCH's Clearing House Committee on October 24 (Clearing House Committee Minutes, October 24, 1907).

The Morgan initiatives generated nothing but unqualified praise from his contemporaries and later from historians and biographers of the leading participants. Sprague (1910, pp. 257–58) alone expressed reservations: "Had clearing-house loan certificates been issued early in the week, it would not have been necessary to resort to the cumbersome device of money pools, liquidation of the stock exchange would have been somewhat less, and the alarm, to which the sudden fall in security prices contributed, would have been in part escaped." Evidence not available at the time Sprague wrote suggests that Morgan made the serious error of allowing the Knickerbocker Trust to fail, thereby exacerbating the panic. Moreover, his partner George Perkins allegedly bore some responsibility for the run on the Trust Company of America by announcing to the press the night before that the "sore point" the next day would be the Trust Company of America, tending to concentrate depositor unrest on a single institution. Morgan's money pooling arrangements to aid the Trust Company of America, the Lincoln Trust, and other smaller trust companies did not put an end to massive deposit withdrawals which continued for at least two weeks, though it allowed them to avoid closure. The Morgan initiatives did not immediately restore depositor confidence nor terminate frantic depositor withdrawals, as Clearing House action had done in previous panics. The reputation of Morgan did not match that of the NYCH. Money pooling was not an efficient substitute for NYCH collective action.

The behavior of the NYCH can also be faulted for the delay in the issue of clearing house loan certificates and in resorting at the same time to the suspension of cash payments. Reserves at no time had reached the point where suspension was inevitable. There was little or no change in total reserves following the first panic week. The resumption of cash payments was delayed for two months not because of an inadequate level of total reserves but because of the continued existence of a large reserve deficit.

Institutional failure and not the absence of effective control instruments, Sprague concluded almost ninety years ago, was the major cause of the 1907 panic. The NYCH failed to grasp the fact that its responsibilities for banking stability extended not only to its own members but to all banks – trust companies and state and national bank nonmembers. Narrow, self-serving considerations prevented the NYCH from coming to the aid of the Knickerbocker Trust which, if it had been a member of Clearing House, undoubtedly would have received direct financial support.

In the first section of this chapter, I construct original estimates of the number and geographical distribution of bank failures both for New York and the interior during the panic months. The second section consists of a brief narrative account of what happened during the three stages of the banking unrest. The role of the U.S. Treasury and gold imports during the panic are explored in the third section. Hoarding as a panic phenomenon is discussed in the fourth section, including the emergence of a currency premium. The behavior of reserves, loans, and deposits of NYCH banks and the trust companies is the subject of the fifth section. Measures of the real effects of the panic are contained in the sixth section. The seventh section addresses the question of institutional failure as a fundamental cause of the 1907 panic, and the final section provides a short summary of what this chapter has attempted to accomplish.

Bank Suspensions and Their Geographical Distribution

Our estimates of the number and geographical distribution of bank failures during the panics of 1873, 1884, and 1890 revealed how few they actually were in both New York and the interior. The one notable exception was 1893 when the number of suspensions rivaled the panics of the Great Depression. The 1907 bank failure experience, as we see below, resembled the earlier panics, but interestingly enough the deposits of failed banks were greater than in 1893, thus reinforcing our conclusion that bank closings per se were not a reliable guide to the severity of banking panics nor did they provide a good description of what happened during banking panics. Estimates of the number and geographical distribution of bank closures including trust companies, savings banks, and brokerage firms (private banks) are shown in Tables 5.1 and 5.2. These estimates were constructed from individual bank suspension announcements listed in financial journals and newspapers during the three months October through December. Though the panic reached its zenith in October, the number of bank suspensions remained high in the two succeeding months.

Table 5.1. *Number of bank suspensions in New York and Interior, October–December 1907*

	New York	Interior	Total
October	13	12	25
November		23	23
December		25	25

Source: Author's estimates.

Table 5.2. *Regional distribution of bank suspensions, October–December 1907*

	October	November	December
Middle Atlantic	15	1	2
Southern		4	4
Western	6	10	13
Northwestern	1	1	
Pacific	1	5	5
Territories: Northeast	2	2	1
Total	25	23	25

It is clear from Table 5.1 that the total number of bank closings was relatively small and about equally divided between New York and the interior during the panic month of October. In November and December there were no failures in New York. However, the number of failures remained high in the interior. Bank failures in the interior during October were negligible, the two largest of which were the Union Trust of Providence, Rhode Island, with deposits of $25.4 million and the California Safe Deposit and Trust Company with deposits of $9 million on October 31. Banking holidays were declared in Oklahoma on the 28th, in Washington and Oregon on the 29th, and in California on the 31st. The city of Newark, New Jersey, declared a three-day banking holiday on the 24th.

The high concentration of bank failures in New York during the panic month of October accounts for the dominant role of the Middle Atlantic region (Table 5.2). In November and December the largest number of suspensions occurred in the Western region (mainly the present-day

Table 5.3. *Bank suspensions by bank classification, October–December 1907*

	National	State	Private	Savings	Trust	Total
October	1	7	6	2	9	25
November	7	12	1		3	23
December	3	14	3	2	3	25

Midwest), with 40 percent in November and over 50 percent in December. The South and West accounted for 60 percent in November and 68 percent in December. The Northeastern region suffered the least. Table 5.3 shows the distribution of bank suspensions by bank classification. One-third of the bank suspensions in October were trust companies and another one-third state banks. The total number of bank closings was about the same in the panic and two post-panic months.

Bradstreet's provides monthly estimates of the total number of business failures and total liabilities inclusive of failures of financial institutions. But the monthly estimates do not always separate bank closures from commercial business suspensions. Fortunately, the separation is made for October. Of the 964 business failures in October 1907, twenty represented failures of financial institutions. My own estimate is twenty-five. The liabilities of the twenty banking firms that closed amounted to $120 million, 86 percent of the total liabilities of all business suspensions. Four-fifths of these liabilities were in New York City, and three-fifths of that total were liabilities of trust companies. There are no estimates for total deposits. There were eighty-nine financial failures in the year 1907 with total liabilities of $206 million. Three out of four were in the final quarter, or sixty-six. My estimate is somewhat greater – seventy-three – and nearly 90 percent of all liabilities of failed institutions occurred in the final quarter.

The suspensions in 1907 were only a fraction of the bank closures in 1893. But – and this is especially important – total liabilities of failed banks were over 20 percent greater in 1907 than in 1893! In 1907 seventeen trust companies failed with 57 percent of total liabilities of failed financial institutions. Though the number of bank suspensions was small in 1907, the liabilities of these few banks were especially large.

The small number and geographical specificity of bank failures in the interior cannot explain how the panic was transmitted from New York to the rest of the country. The partial suspension of cash payment first by the NYCH and followed immediately by clearing houses in the

interior was the shock that the general public experienced, not bank closings. A. Piatt Andrew (1908a) solicited responses from 145 of the largest
cities, of which seventy-one resorted to the use of loan certificates, clearing house checks, or other money substitutes, and in twenty other cities
the banks' largest depositors were requested to mark their checks
"payable only through the clearing house." All told, in two-thirds of the
cities with a population of more than 25,000 payment was partially suspended. Partial suspension of cash payment disrupted the payments
mechanism by sharply increasing the costs of currency transactions.
The average citizen experienced directly the effects of the panic not
by having observed bank runs and bank closures but by suffering the
inconvenience of sharply curtailed deposit-using transactions and in
some instances a currency shortage.

Bank Panic Narrative

There were three stages of the banking crisis in 1907. One was a pre-
panic stage involving at least eight New York City banks with deposits
of over $70 million, which was sparked by an unsuccessful attempt to
corner the copper market. The crisis was bank-specific and confined to
those banks whose officials participated in the copper corner or were
associated one way or another with those who did. There was no general
loss of depositor confidence. The reason why there was no panic was
that the New York Clearing House intervened immediately by offering
either direct support or by organizing support for the troubled banks,
thereby forestalling further banking unrest. This first stage was met in an
exemplary manner, and the crisis would probably have been over had
not depositor uncertainty spread to the trust companies who were not
members of NYCH.

The second stage of the banking panic proper began with a run on the
Knickerbocker Trust and spread quickly to the Trust Company of
America and the Lincoln Trust. During this stage the NYCH remained
in the background, and J. P. Morgan took charge of the efforts being
made to come to the aid of the trust companies in distress. These efforts
were successful in keeping the trust companies open but less successful
in terminating immediately depositor withdrawals.

The third stage was initiated by the impending threat of the failure of
the brokerage firm of Moore and Schley and ended when the firm was
bailed out by a Morgan initiative which entailed the purchase of shares
of the Tennessee Coal and Iron Company in exchange for U.S. Steel 5
percent mortgage bonds. Each stage of the disturbance is examined in
turn.

The First Stage

The first stage of the banking disturbance was precipitated by a bold but unsuccessful attempt by Augustus Heinze and his associates to corner the mining stock of the United Copper Company. When the scheme collapsed on October 16, 1907, two brokerage houses – Gross and Kleeburg and Otto Heinze and Company – that were directly involved in stock manipulation failed. Runs immediately ensued on three banks whose officers and directors were connected to the copper corner: Mercantile National Bank, New Amsterdam Bank, and the National Bank of North America, with deposits of $11.6 million, $5.1 million, and $13.3 million respectively. Augustus Heinze was president of Mercantile National, of which C. F. Morse was a director. Morse controlled the National Bank of North America and was a director of the Mechanics' and Traders Bank. The Thomas brothers owned the Consolidated National Bank with which the Heinzes were associated; they were also involved in the management of the Hamilton Bank and the Hudson Trust Company. All parties had interests in the Amsterdam National Bank and the Fourteenth Street Bank. The Heinze-Morse-Thomas brothers' banks and their deposits are shown below:

Mercantile (NYCH member)	$11.6 million
Consolidated National	3.9
National Bank of North America (NYCH member)	13.3
Mechanics and Traders Bank (NYCH member)	19.0
New Amsterdam National Bank (NYCH member)	5.1
Fourteenth Street Bank (NYCH member)	7.4
Hamilton Bank	7.2
Hudson Trust Company	3.8
	$71.4

The collapse of the copper corner eroded depositor confidence in these banks with strong ties to Augustus Heinze and his associates and posed the danger of spreading to other banks as well.

The immediate response of the NYCH was bank-specific, as it had been in the case of the Metropolitan Bank in 1884 and the Bank of North America in 1890. The decision was made to treat separately each of the three problem banks. During the first stage of the 1907 panic no thought was given to authorizing the issue of clearing house certificates. On October 17, Heinze resigned as president of the Mercantile National Bank. The State Savings Bank of Butte, Montana, with deposits of $4 million, of which he was the leading shareholder, suspended. The next day the NYCH conducted an examination of the Mercantile National and found it to be solvent. The Clearing House Committee voted to make available whatever amount of cash that would be needed. Mercantile's debit balance at the Clearing House for that day was $745,000, $400,000 of which was promptly paid by the committee. A condition for assistance was the resignation of every director; the committee regarded as one of its first tasks in addition to providing financial assistance the complete reorganization of the bank. The NYCH also acted as a catalyst for obtaining $1.9 million from a syndicate of nine Clearing House banks, each of whom contributed $200,000. On October 18 $400,000 was advanced to Mercantile, and on October 19, $900,000.

On October 19 and 20 the Clearing House Committee extended its examinations to the National Bank of North America and the New Amsterdam National Bank, both of which were declared solvent. Arrangements were made by the committee for two Clearing House banks to supply a $10 million fund to aid the three banks. Mercantile National received $1.9 million on Monday, October 21; the New Amsterdam National Bank received $300,000 on the following day to discharge its debt to the NYCH. Both were able to meet their Clearing House indebtedness on Wednesday and Thursday. The Clearing House insisted that Heinze, Morse, and the Thomas brothers withdraw from all association with banks receiving their support. No assistance was given to the Bank of North America, since the bank's directors were able to raise $1.75 million on their own initiative.

On October 19 the Mercantile National Bank had given notice that it would no longer clear for the Hamilton Bank after Monday, October 21. A run occurred on the bank on Wednesday and Thursday, and it was forced to close along with the Twelfth Ward Bank.

The Second Stage

The second stage of the banking disturbance began on Tuesday, October 22, with runs on the Knickerbocker Trust (see Tallman and Moen, 1990), the Trust Company of America, and the National Bank of North America. The disturbance was not unanticipated. Fears had been expressed over the previous weekend by bank and trust company officials that there might be a renewal of banking unrest on October 21. On that day the president of the National Bank of Commerce, V. P. Snyder, appeared before the Clearing House committee (Minutes, October 21, 1907) with the third vice president of Knickerbocker Trust, who explained to the committee the condition of his bank and requested a loan. After due deliberation the committee concluded: "The Knicker-bocker Trust Company, having requested a loan from the Clearing House, it was decided that the advance of money for the protection of depositors is limited to its own members."

J. P. Morgan had returned from a religious conference in Richmond, Virginia, at the request made earlier in the week by his associates in New York. A conference of leading bankers was held on Sunday in the Morgan Library where it was decided that the banks and trust com-panies should cooperate to save solvent banking institutions. A commit-tee was selected to review the solvency of those banks seeking financial assistance.

On Monday the directors of the Knickerbocker Trust called for the resignation of its president, Charles T. Barney. He had been involved with some of the Morse ventures. And the National Bank of Commerce announced that it would no longer clear for Knickerbocker. That evening the Knickerbocker directors requested help from the Morgan group.

Almost immediately the committee appointed to evaluate the sol-vency of troubled banks convened to examine the Knickerbocker Trust and to ascertain its solvency. The committee was headed by Benjamin Strong, a vice president at Bankers Trust who later became the distin-guished governor of the Federal Reserve Bank of New York. The results of that investigation had an important bearing on why support was not made available to the Knickerbocker Trust. If it had been, the panic may have taken an altogether different course. Satterlee (1939, p. 464), Morgan's biographer, claimed that Morgan felt the closing of Knicker-bocker was inevitable, and Henry Davison, a close advisor to Morgan, was convinced by Strong's investigation that the Knickerbocker was not solvent.

Since the judgment of both supposedly depended on the facts un-covered by Strong, it is especially important that we understand what Strong's investigation did and did not do. Chandler (1958, p. 28) has stated: "It was on the basis of Strong's reports that Morgan and his asso-ciates decided whether to save the various stricken financial institutions." Strong prepared a first hand account of what happened during these critical days in the form of a 22-page letter that he wrote to Thomas Lamont in 1924 and which was quoted extensively by Chandler. Chan-dler (1958, p. 28), apparently following Satterlee (1939, p. 75), concluded that Knickerbocker closed on the same day the investigation by Strong had begun "before even a cursory examination could be completed." Satterlee gave as the reason that its free assets available for a loan were too limited to afford time for a plan to be worked out. Strong told Lamont (Chandler, 1958, p. 28): "That night I went home to Greenwich with a deep feeling of apprehension lest we were facing a real disaster, and especially anxious because of our impotence to do anything for the relief of the Knickerbocker Trust Company."

What seems to be clear from the available record is that Strong did not at any time report either to Davison or to Morgan that the conclusion of his committee was that the Knickerbocker was insolvent; the investigation had not proceeded that far. Liquid resources may have been inadequate to warrant a loan, but that says nothing about whether the Knickerbocker was solvent or not. It is indeed curious that Morgan concluded that the trust company was insolvent since he took such pride in not getting involved with details of the individual case and accepting the judgment of his trusted colleagues which he did in all subsequent requests for support. The time factor was critical. If adequate securities could have been located quickly to act as collateral for a loan, support would almost surely have been forthcoming; it probably did not matter that much whether the bank was solvent or not given the nature of the emergency.

That Knickerbocker was not hopelessly insolvent was evident from the fact that the bank reopened on March 26, 1908, with assets of $52 million and a surplus of $14 million. There was an infusion of a $2.4 million from stockholders and an additional $13 million collected by receivers from the disposal of assets.

Failure to have prevented the collapse of the Knickerbocker Trust was perhaps an understandable error of judgment on the part of the NYCH and Morgan and his chief advisors. It simply exacerbated depositor unrest in the Trust Company of America on Wednesday. For the want of a few million dollars to sustain Knickerbocker, the Morgan group eventually had to put out well over $40 million to keep the trust companies in New York City open.

The run on the Trust Company of America, the third largest with deposits of $48 million, allegedly was aggravated on Tuesday evening by a public statement attributed to George W. Perkins, a senior Morgan partner, who attempted to summarize the results of the deliberations of the Morgan group. He allegedly stated that the Trust Company of America was the "sore point," and this was repeated Wednesday morning in the *New York Times*. Allen (1949, p. 248) concluded that the run on the Trust Company of America was the result of Perkins's injudicious statement. The Associated Press considered it too volatile to print. The president of the Trust Company of America thought that the "sore point" statement caused the run on his bank, since withdrawals on Tuesday had amounted only to $500,000 and on Wednesday to $13 million. In testimony before the Stanley Committee (U.S. House of Representatives,

1911, pp. 1503–8) Perkins steadfastly denied having made such a statement. It would be interesting to speculate whether Perkins's gaffe cost him his job as a Morgan partner. His ten-year contract terminated soon after the panic, and was not renewed.

The initiative to aid the Trust Company of America came primarily from J. P. Morgan, who was in almost continuous consultation with his associates, who were keeping close tab on the developing crisis. He was prepared to extend a sizable loan to the Trust Company on the collateral of a portfolio of its best securities, the proceeds of which he obtained from the First National and National City banks representing a group, though not specified, of other NYCH banks. The NYCH was not directly involved in the negotiations.

At the same time Morgan invited the presidents of all the trust companies to meet in his office. Trust company officials had no organization to represent their interests, and Satterlee reported (1939, p. 461) that "many of them were strangers to one another and had to be introduced." Without leadership of any kind and no organizational framework, initiative could hardly have been expected. Morgan attempted to fill the void by having them select a committee to act for them all.

In the meantime Strong reported that the Trust Company of America was solvent and that it would be safe to make a loan to the trust company. But from what Strong later wrote to Lamont (1933, p. 76) about his examination, one would have to conclude that the condition of the bank was one of borderline solvency at best:

> I told Mr. Morgan that I was satisfied that the Trust Company of America was solvent; and I thought its surplus had been pretty much wiped out; but that the capital was not greatly impaired, if at all, although, were the company to be liquidated, there were many assets which it would take some years finally to convert to cash.

On Tuesday night Morgan agreed to loan $1 million to the Trust Company. National City and First National Banks provided an additional $2.5 million on the 23rd.

On Wednesday evening Morgan convened another meeting of the trust company officials, explained to them the necessity of extending more aid to the Trust Company of America, and recommended that they raise $10 million on their own to be available the next morning. Although the trust company presidents were reluctant to advance the funds, they pledged $8.5 million, the difference being made up by Morgan's Bank, First National, National City, and the Hanover National banks. The Union Trust Company acted as the agent for the dispersal of the funds. It disbursed $6.9 million on the 24th, $2.15 million on the 25th, $180,000 on the 26th, $590,000 on the 28th, $100,000 on the 30th, and the rest on the 31st.

A suggestion was also made at the Wednesday evening meeting that an appeal ought to be made to the Secretary of the Treasury for assistance. Perkins (U.S. House of Representatives, 1911, p. 1774) went to the Secretary's room at the Manhattan Hotel where the plan was devised for the Secretary to deposit $25 million with three national banks on the next day.

On Thursday John D. Rockefeller deposited $10 million in the Union Trust with deposits of $40 million to support the bank, if needed. Pandemonium broke out at the Stock Exchange with call money quoted at 100 percent. The president of the exchange informed Morgan that it might be necessary to close the exchange. In a concerted effort to stave off the closing, Morgan obtained the financial support of neighborhood banks, who contributed $27 million to be loaned to the exchange at 10 percent. During the day two banks closed in Harlem: Twelfth Ward and the Hamilton banks, and the Empire 'Savings Bank required notice of withdrawal. Runs continued on the Trust Company of America and the Lincoln Trust.

The presidents of the banks and trust companies met again Thursday evening with Morgan to formulate a further plan of action. The only agreement reached was the desirability of issuing clearing house certificates. Morgan went along reluctantly. According to Satterlee (1939, p. 476) Morgan had always been opposed to the issue of clearing house certificates, and "to issue them would be confession to the world that the banks in New York had not enough currency to carry on their business and that the very fact of issuing them would further disturb banking and business conditions. . . ."

Runs on the Trust Company of America and Lincoln Trust continued on Friday. Additional funds were made available to both banks. And the situation on the stock exchange had not improved. At a meeting called by Morgan, he succeeded in raising an additional $13 million for the exchange. Seven banks failed, four of which were located in Brooklyn. And the thirty-two New York savings banks required notice of withdrawal. Ten banks had failed in the preceding three days. The names of the banks, dates of closure, and dates normal operations were resumed are given in Table 5.4.

The fact that all but two resumed normal operations within eight months indicated that they were probably solvent at the time of closure. On Saturday the NYCH finally decided to authorize the issue of clearing house certificates to be effective Monday, October 28; cash payment was also suspended. However, the panic was not over. Runs on the two

Table 5.4. *Ten bank failures in three days*

	Date of closure	Date of resumption
Knickerbocker Trust	October 22, 1907	March 26, 1908
Hamilton Bank	October 24, 1907	January 20, 1908
Twelfth Ward Bank	October 24, 1907	November 20, 1907
United Exchange Bank	October 25, 1907	November 25, 1907
Brooklyn Bank in the City of New York	October 25, 1907	June 23, 1908
Borough Bank of Brooklyn	October 25, 1907	April 14, 1908
International Trust Company	October 25, 1907	
Jenkins Trust Company of Brooklyn	October 25, 1907	April 14, 1908
Williamsburg Trust Company of Brooklyn	October 25, 1907	
Terminal Bank of Brooklyn	October 25, 1907	November 2, 1907

trust companies continued. Another $15 million would be necessary to sustain the Trust Company of America. On November 1, Benjamin Strong's committee undertook a second examination of the Trust Company of America to determine whether adequate collateral still existed. He made his report on the following evening to the trust company officials assembled in the Morgan Library. The equity of the trust company he found to be about $2 million, a much less pessimistic estimate than that given in the committee's initial examination. The trust company presidents were once again reluctant to act, but Morgan persisted and the necessary funds were raised. Without the unremitting pressure of Morgan, the trust companies would have done nothing and the situation would have deteriorated further.

The Third Stage

The third and final stage of the 1907 panic and the most controversial of Morgan's initiatives began on Friday, November 1, with the threatened suspension of the New York brokerage house of Moore and Schley. The ramifications of the closure were too ominous to ignore. The firm had borrowed heavily on time loans which were to fall due on the following Monday with little or no prospects for renewal; it had also used Tennessee Coal and Iron (TC&I) company shares as collateral for bank loans in New York, Chicago, Philadelphia, and Boston. What complicated the situation was that the TC&I certificates were not owned by Moore and Schley but were collateral for money borrowed by Moore and Schley by the purchasers of TC&I stock which in turn was used by Moore and Schley as collateral for bank loans. The banks to whom Moore and Schley were indebted were pressing the brokerage firm to substitute more liquid stocks for the TC&I shares; the market for TC&I shares was exceptionally thin and subject to wide fluctuations in price even if a small number of shares were sold in the market, hence the reluctance of the banks to hold their shares as collateral for loans.

The seriousness of the situation was not underestimated by Morgan. He is reported to have said (U.S. House of Representatives [Stanley Hearings], 1911, vol. 2, p. 936): "It is very serious. If Moore and Schley go there is no telling what the effect on Wall Street will be and on financial institutions of New York, and how many other houses will drop with it, and how many banks might be included in the consequences." He thought nothing more serious had arisen during the course of the panic. Morgan's sentiments were echoed by Strong (Lamont, 1933, p. 77), who maintained that the real crisis of 1907 panic began on the same day when it became known that the brokerage house of Moore and Schley might be forced into bankruptcy because of a sharp decline in the shares of TC&I.

A novel plan was devised to which Morgan gave his approval. The U.S. Steel Corporation would purchase the majority of the TC&I stock, and in exchange the holders of the stock would receive U.S. Steel 5 percent mortgage bonds: one share of TC&I stock exchanging for one U.S. Steel bond. How then did the exchange of TC&I shares for U.S. Steel mortgage bonds keep Moore and Schley from failing? Schley (U.S. House of Representatives, 1911, pp. 1084–85) testified that he sold 53,000 shares for U.S. Steel mortgage bonds belonging to himself and another investor that were worth $12 million which was used to pay off their indebtedness to Moore and Schley; the brokerage firm in turn used the proceeds of the debt repayment to liquidate its bank indebtedness. Thus the brokerage firm avoided closure, and the threat of a renewal of the panic was over in substance. The agreement to exchange TC&I shares for U.S. Steel mortgage bonds also included the important provision whereby the banks would guarantee support for the trust companies to prevent their closure.

The Morgan scheme to save Moore and Schley did not escape criticism. In 1911 Congress conducted a full-scale investigation of the circumstances under which U.S. Steel acquired control of TC&I (U.S. House of Representatives, 1911). In acquiring TC&I did U.S. Steel violate the provisions of the Sherman Antitrust Act? The chief investigator wanted to know whether any alternatives to U.S. Steel control were considered, though he did not question the propriety of saving the brokerage firm. The acquisition smacked of a not-so-subtle attempt by U.S. Steel to increase its monopoly power. For our purposes the Stanley Hearings are an indispensable source for what happened during the Moore and Schley episode. What can we say about the Morgan initiative to save Moore and Schley? It was clearly successful, though a clumsy preventive device indicative of what happened when leadership during a banking panic is relinquished for whatever reason by the NYCH and for which is substituted the ad hoc initiative of a charismatic banking leader.

Confidence was not restored before November 6 when a plan finally emerged to salvage the two trust companies. Some 66 percent of the stock of each company was placed in the hands of a voting trustee, and the stock was used as collateral to borrow from a syndicate of trust companies sufficient to meet their daily needs for cash. The Trust Company of America received $15 million which was disbursed over a period beginning November 6 and continuing through February 4, 1908.

Sprague (1910, pp. 255–56) concluded that the funds supplied to the two trust companies "served no purpose of general importance. If it had been used to meet the demands of the banks throughout the country, alarm might possibly have been delayed and suspension avoided." Support by the Morgan syndicate was only partially successful "because they lacked the authority and backing of the Clearing House Association." Moreover, the effort lacked credibility since there was no commitment that support would continue. Money pools to Sprague were no substitute for clearing house action. The failure of the NYCH to issue loan certificates as early as October 15 or 16 was the most serious error made during the crisis (Sprague, 1910, p. 257), and "had clearing house loan certificates been issued early in the week it would not have been necessary to resort to the cumbersome device of money pools."

The New York Clearing House loan committee (Minutes, January 13, 1908) explained their failure to have authorized the issue of loan certificates earlier as follows:

It had been hoped that the crisis imminent for a week previous might be successfully met without the necessity for the issuance of Clearing House Loan Certificates, in spite of the urgent application for assistance from several bank members of the Association.

The committee had placed too much faith in the joint action of several of the banks in advancing cash to specific troubled banks, not including the trust companies under siege by the depositors.

Another reason, we can only speculate, was Morgan's negative attitude toward the issue of loan certificates. He had the opportunity to express his views when he was invited to attend the Clearing House committee called to discuss this matter. According to his son-in-law and biographer (Satterlee, 1939, p. 267), "There is no record of just what Mr. Morgan did in this [1893] panic." But we have explained his role in the 1890 panic. What he learned, if anything, from previous panics, is not at all clear. But in 1907 his two closest associates during the crisis were George Baker of First National Bank and James Stillman of National City Bank, and both deferred to his leadership. Stillman had just completed his term on October 1 as chairman of the NYCH executive committee, the policy-making body of the Clearing House. He was in the best position to influence NYCH action. His biographer Anna Burr (1927, p. 232) has stated that Stillman worked closely with his successor James Woodward, the head of Hanover National Bank. She also said he worked in "close harmony" with Morgan, "deferring to him as was his custom and fully appreciating that the two great groups represented by himself and Morgan should move in this crisis as one." Such close harmony apparently accounts for the inaction of the NYCH.

However, Stillman was not unwilling to challenge Morgan. On the issue of aid to the smaller trust companies, he had a strong difference of opinion with him (Burr, 1927, pp. 273 ff.). Morgan did not intend to support them. Stillman disagreed but did not give any reasons. Burr conjectured that Stillman feared that these smaller institutions might fall into the hands of a rival financial power. Nevertheless, Stillman carried the day and support was provided to the smaller trust companies. Morgan's authority could be breeched without jeopardizing the spirit of cooperation between them.

All told, more than $100 million was raised at Morgan's initiative to keep the panic from getting worse; it included $30 million to the stock exchange, $30 million to New York City to prevent debt default, and a large indeterminate amount to rescue twelve financial institutions, most of which were trust companies. The piecemeal aid to the trust companies did not restore depositor confidence. The Trust Company of American, for example, lost over $30 million in deposits between October 22, 1907, and February, 1908.

Role of the U.S. Treasury and Gold Imports

The U.S. Treasury played a key role in supplementing Morgan's plan to support the troubled trust companies. Without Treasury deposits of currency in select New York banks, the trust companies would have been unable to obtain the currency necessary from the national banks to meet urgent deposit withdrawals. But Treasury support was a one-shot affair. After the initial injection of funds, its resources were exhausted.

Table 5.5. *Government deposits at three New York banks, October 19 and 31, 1907 (in millions of dollars)*

	October 19	October 23	Change
Hanover	4.9	10.3	5.4
National City	5.4	14.7	9.3
First National	2.0	11.3	24
Total	12.3	36.3	24

Source: U.S. Senate, 1908, p. 57.

Additional measures, however, were taken to increase the bank note circulation.

On October 22, Secretary of the Treasury George Cortelyou came to New York for the explicit purpose of providing assistance to the troubled banks. From an office in the Subtreasury he collected the information necessary to understand the current crisis. He subsequently consulted with George Perkins, a Morgan partner, and together they discussed the amount of assistance to be made available. On Wednesday at a meeting of the trust company presidents, Morgan told them (Satterlee, 1939, p. 472) that Secretary Cortelyou was in New York and was prepared to deposit funds in select national banks to insure that adequate funds would be available to meet depositor demands for cash the next day. Cortelyou deposited $25 million on Thursday. By the end of the week a total of $35 million had been placed at the banks' disposal. Table 5.5 shows the increase in government deposits between October 19 and 31 at three of the largest national banks. It is clear that nearly 70 percent of the deposits were placed in the three banks, the reason being that these banks would be providing the bulk of the cash through the withdrawal of trust company balances needed to satisfy depositor demands.

The Treasury also made deposits in banks in Chicago ($3 million), Pittsburgh ($1.5 million), Cincinnati ($1.5 million), Minneapolis and St. Paul ($500,000), and other places in the South and the West. By mid-November the Treasury had utilized all nonoperating funds available, even to the extent of reducing its working balance to around $5 million. Two additional measures were taken that had the effect of increasing the circulation of national bank notes. National banks were permitted to substitute bonds suitable for savings bank investments for government bonds which were held as security against public deposits, thereby freeing government bonds to secure an increased bank note circulation. And on November 17 subscriptions were invited for $50 million of Panama Canal bonds and $100 million of 3 percent certificates of indebtedness. Banks to which Panama Canal bonds were sold could retain 90 percent of the purchase price as a deposit and 75 percent if they were certificates of deposit. Some $25 million dollars of Panama Canal bonds were subscribed and $15 million of certificates, nearly all of which was used either to increase the note circulation or to secure public deposits. The total increase in bank note circulation between August 22 and December 3 was approximately $16 million.

Gold imports, though an important source of reserves, did not arrive in time to be of much use in the panic weeks of October, nor did they shorten the period of cash suspension. During the week beginning Monday, October 28, exchange rates turned favorable and $25 million of gold was engaged for import, though that gold did not arrive until November. The following week exchange rates moved well above the gold export point, but gold continued to come in. Gold imports amounted to $58 million in November and $38 million in December, for a grand total of $96 million. Sprague (1910, p. 283) attributed the high rate of exchange to the currency premium; however, he did not think that it was the cause of gold imports. The export surplus monthly from August to December is shown below:

August	$1.5 million
September	2.9
October	68.0
November	93.5
December	114.9

Imports were lower in December than at any other time in the past five years, and exports were twice their normal amount.

We might have expected such large gold inflows in November and December to have shortened the period of suspension of cash payment as reserves accumulated in New York banks. That did not happen. New York continued to make large shipments of cash to the interior: more than $106 million between October 26 and December. Sprague (1910, p. 186) concluded that the gold flowed to the interior as a result of large commodity exports by the South and the West.

Hoarding

Unlike in previous panics, monthly data exist on currency held by the public, vault cash, the ratio of deposits to bank reserves, and the ratio of

Table 5.6. *Currency held by the public, vault cash, and the ratio of deposits to reserve and deposits to currency, August–December 1907**

	Currency held by public (millions of dollars)	Vault cash (millions of dollars)	Ratio of deposits to reserves	Ratio of deposits to currency
August	1,654	1,164	8.5	5.98
September	1,631	1,184	8.23	5.97
October	1,730	1,155	8.20	5.51
November	1,784	1,205	7.78	5.25
December	1,861	1,208	7.60	4.93

Source: Friedman and Schwartz, 1963, pp. 706, 800.
* Data are seasonally adjusted.

deposits to currency held by the public, and are set out in Table 5.6. Currency held by the public increased 6.1 percent between September and the panic month of October. This compares with an increase of 2.2 and 5.8 percent for the corresponding panic months in 1930 and 1931 during the Great Depression. The deposit to currency ratio fell 7.7 percent between September and October and more than 17 percent between September and December.

A. Piatt Andrew (1908), a contemporary student of the 1907 panic, attempted to obtain evidence on the amount of increase in the public's holdings of currency in the absence of any official data by obtaining information on new deposit rentals from seventeen safe deposit companies across the country: nine in New York, three in St. Louis, two in Boston, two in San Francisco, and one in Chicago. It was a clever research strategy without scientific pretensions but perhaps better than crude subjective inference. He concluded, contrary to the conventional wisdom, that the increase in new safe deposit rentals was attributable to large business interests rather than to small depositors, and that the transfer was less extensive in the interior than in New York for the reason that the panic had not assumed very serious dimensions before the banks suspended cash payments. Monthly data on currency held by the public cannot address the issue of the distribution of currency between business firms and individuals. Nor can it say anything about geographical incidence.

Both Andrew and Friedman and Schwartz observed that the increase in hoarding was due less to the loss of depositor confidence than to the loss of confidence by country banks. Between August 22, the nearest call date to the October panic, and December 3, the cash holdings of country banks had increased by $48 million; reserve city bank cash holdings decreased by $27.7 million and central reserve city holdings by $59.6 million.

Why did the cash holdings of the country banks increase? There are at least three plausible reasons: (1) Past experience had taught them that money was difficult to obtain from reserve city banks in times of panic; (2) distrust of other banks generated unreasonable fear; and (3) there was an inadequacy of reserves at the beginning of the panic. Sprague (1910, p. 307) concluded that all three considerations played a role, but the principal reason, he conjectured, was the inadequacy of the cash reserve at the outset. Elsewhere he had emphasized that banks lacked confidence in each other: "Everywhere the banks suddenly found themselves confronted with demands for money by frightened depositors; everywhere, also, banks manifested a lack of confidence in each other. . . . The evidence of lack of confidence in and between the banks is clear and points to serious difficulty in carrying on banking in this country" (Sprague, 1910, p. 259). Friedman and Schwartz (1963, pp. 16–20) also noted that "although there were runs on some banks in scattered parts of the country due to local causes, loss of confidence was displayed less by the public than by the country banks." And they attributed the increase to the first of Sprague's three plausible reasons: Past experience had taught the banks that money was difficult to obtain from reserve city and central reserve city banks in times of panic.

Andrew (1908, p. 297) observed the cash reserve ratios held by the banks outside the central reserve cities both before and during the panic; the data showed that they had accumulated excess reserves of cash which they were loathe to part with at the height of the panic. He did not think that this simply represented "traditionally conservative policy . . . but a sudden and frightened effort to protect themselves from impending trouble." And, again, "a large number of bankers, especially in the West and South, appear to have become panic-stricken along with the general public, and to have adopted the fatal policy of *sauve qui peut*."

Andrew, Sprague, and Friedman and Schwartz all agreed that panic-stricken country banks together with the loss of depositor's confidence were largely responsible for the increase in hoarding. It could be argued with some plausibility that the country banks should have prepared for just such a contingency by holding surplus reserves in their own vaults. If they had, we could expect that their cash holdings would have been drawn down rather than increased! Their reserve percentage increased from 7.6 percent on August 22 to 9.9 percent on December 3. According to Sprague (1910, pp. 304–5) this slight increase was entirely in accord with precedent, although at the time it was regarded as unusual; they needed additional supplies of cash to meet the demands of depositors before suspension, and even after suspension of cash payment they attempted to withdraw as much cash as possible from reserve agents. We are not able to determine how much of the increase in currency holdings by country banks occurred before suspension and how much thereafter. If the greater part occurred after suspension, then we might infer that the demands of depositors was not particularly important in either New York or the interior. The absence of more detailed data does not warrant any strong inference about the relative significance of currency holding by depositors and country banks.

As we have seen in our previous discussion of the 1873 and 1893 panics, when cash payments were suspended a currency premium immediately arose. Data on the currency premium in New York are given in Table 5.7 beginning October 31 and continuing through December 31. The discontinuance of the premium coincided with the resumption of cash payment by the NYCH banks in early January.

Presumably the effect of the currency premium was to return currency from hoards, but how successful it was cannot be determined because of the absence of data. The effect of the currency premium in reducing hoarding may have been offset by the increased desire to hold cash associated with the cessation of cash payment. The amount of cash required for a given volume of transactions inevitably increased with the sharp contraction in deposit-using transactions.

Behavior of Reserves, Loans, and Deposits of NYCH Banks and Trust Companies

The best single measure of the condition of the New York banks is the behavior of total reserves – gold plus legal tender currency. Their ability to sustain cash payment rests on the size and distribution of the cash reserve. As we show, when the NYCH suspended payment total reserves were more than adequate. Why the NYCH decided to couple the authorization to issue clearing house certificates with the suspension of cash payment when there was an adequate cash reserve can be explained by the greater importance the Clearing House committee attached to the reserve ratio as a guide to their behavior. The focus of the committee was not on total cash reserves but on the size of the reserve deficit, which also explains why the committee waited so long to restore cash payments.

Table 5.7. *Currency premium in the 1907 panic*

	Currency premium			Currency premium	
	High percent	Low percent		High percent	Low percent
Oct. 31	3	2	Dec. 1	(b)	(b)
Nov. 1	$3\frac{1}{2}$	2	2	$1\frac{1}{4}$	1
2	3	2	3	2	—
3	(b)	(b)	4	$1\frac{3}{4}$	$\frac{3}{4}$
4	$3\frac{1}{2}$	3	5	$1\frac{1}{2}$	$\frac{3}{4}$
5	(a)	(a)	6	1	$\frac{3}{4}$
6	4	2	7	$1\frac{1}{8}$	$\frac{3}{8}$
7	$2\frac{3}{4}$	3	8	(b)	(b)
8	3	2	9	—	—
9	3	—	10	—	—
10	(b)	(b)	11	1	—
11	3	$2\frac{3}{4}$	12	1	—
12	4	$2\frac{3}{4}$	13	$1\frac{1}{2}$	$\frac{3}{4}$
13	4	$3\frac{1}{2}$	14	—	$\frac{1}{2}$
14	3	$2\frac{1}{2}$	15	(b)	(b)
15	$2\frac{1}{2}$	2	16	$1\frac{1}{4}$	$1\frac{1}{8}$
16	2	—	17	$\frac{7}{8}$	$\frac{5}{8}$
17	(b)	(b)	18	—	—
18	3	$2\frac{1}{2}$	19	$1\frac{1}{4}$	—
19	$2\frac{1}{4}$	$1\frac{1}{2}$	20	$\frac{7}{8}$	$\frac{3}{4}$
20	3	—	21	—	—
21	$3\frac{1}{2}$	$2\frac{1}{2}$	22	(a)	(a)
22	$2\frac{3}{4}$	$1\frac{1}{2}$	23	—	—
23	$1\frac{1}{4}$	—	24	—	—
24	(b)	(b)	25	(b)	(b)
25	$1\frac{3}{4}$	1	26	—	—
26	$1\frac{3}{4}$	1	27	$\frac{1}{4}$	—
27	—	$\frac{3}{4}$	28	$\frac{1}{8}$	—
28	(c)	(c)	29	(a)	(a)
29	—	—	30	—	—
30	—	—	31	(c)	(c)

Source: Sprague, 1910, pp. 280–282.
(a) Election day; (b) Sunday; (c) Thanksgiving.

Table 5.8. *Loans, net deposits, and reserves for all New York Clearing house banks for October 12, 19, 26, and November 2, 1907 (in millions of dollars)*

	October 12	October 19	October 26	November 2
Loans	1,083	1,098.6	1,087.7	1,148
Net deposits	1,026	1,025.7	1,023.8	1,052
Reserves	261	267.7	254.7	224
Reserve percent		26.5	24.9	
Surplus reserves	4.7	11.2	1.2	−38.8

Source: *Commercial and Financial Chronicle*, vol. 85 (1907).

When the reserve deficit vanished, the suspension of cash payment ceased.

Table 5.8 shows the behavior of select items on the weekly bank statements of the NYCH banks for three dates: October 19, the week prior to the failure of the Knickerbocker Trust, and the two following weeks. Although reserves fell by almost $13 million the first week and $30.7 million the second week, the absolute level of total bank reserves remained well above $200 million. However, the loss would have been much greater had the Treasury not deposited $36 million in three national banks in New York between October 19 and 31. There was no depletion in aggregate reserves warranting the suspension of cash payment. But the distribution of these reserves among the banks was equally if not more important than the aggregate. By 1907, 60 percent of the reserves of the NYCH banks was concentrated in six banks with two of these six – National City and the Bank of Commerce – holding over one-half of the six-bank total.

Table 5.9 shows the behavior of loans, net deposits, and reserves for the six largest clearing house banks. Reserves had declined between October 19 and 26 by only $7.2 million and their combined cash reserve ratio was still above the legal minimum. But the reserve of some may have been more seriously impaired than others. Loans and deposits increased by $24.2 million and $15 million, respectively. Sprague (1910, p. 273) concluded: "The six large banks acting in concert could have sustained the local situation by making loans and at the same time could have supplied the demands of outside banks for money."

Why then did the NYCH banks suspend cash payment? The issue of loan certificates did not require the suspension of payment. In no other

Table 5.9. *Loans, net deposits, and reserves for
six largest Clearing House banks, October 19 and
26, 1907 (in millions of dollars)*

	October 19	October 26
Loans	544.2	568.4
Net deposits	507.4	527.6
Reserve	139.7	132.3
Reserve percent	27.2	25.3

Source: Sprague, 1910, p. 265.

panic of the national banking era did the two events coincide. Although
loan certificates were authorized in the previous four panics, cash
payment was not suspended in 1884 and 1890. There was nothing
inevitable about the suspension of payment. With the possible exception
of 1873, reserves were not depleted nor even near depletion at the time
of suspension. The explanation later given by the president of the NYCH
placed emphasis on the size of the reserve deficit, which he claimed
reached $53 million. Apparently his memory failed him, for there was
still a small surplus when cash payment was suspended. The $53 million
deficit occurred in the statement week following November 2. Previous
NYCH experience revealed that the size of the reserve deficit rather than
excessive reserve depletions motivated the Clearing House committee.
For the statement week ending October 16, the reserve ratio was barely
below the required reserve percentage and surplus reserves amounted
to $1.2 million. One might easily conclude that the Clearing House com-
mittee was responding less to reserve deficit considerations than to a mis-
taken belief that the authorization to issue loan certificates required the
suspension of cash payments.

The Trust Company Response

We know relatively little about the response of the trust companies in
New York to the panic. We have balance sheet information for all trust
companies in New York State taken from the annual reports of the
Superintendent of Banks for separate call dates. And we also have a
statement of condition of each of the New York City trust companies for
the single call date August 22, 1907, computed by the NYCH from the

Table 5.10. *Select balance sheet items for New York state and city trust companies, August 22 and December 19, 1907 (in millions of dollars)*

| | New York State | | | New York City |
	Aug. 22	Dec. 19	Change	August 22
Cash Reserve	59.3	47.4	−11.9	54.3
Loans	735.6	410.3	−313.3	583.0
Stocks and bonds	414.5	341.1	−73.4	346.0
Total reserves	1,364.0	1,002.0	−362.0	1,205.0
Deposits	812.0	544.1	−267.9	692.6

Source: *Bradstreet's*, 1908, p. 55, and Ellis Tallman, who supplied the author with balance sheets of the individual New York City trust companies.

official reports of the Superintendent of Banks. Weekly balance sheet data do not become available before February 1908.

Table 5.10 shows the amount and changes in select balance sheet items for all New York State trust companies at the two separate call dates August 22 and December 19, 1907, and for New York City trust companies on the single date August 22.

On August 22, 1907, there were twelve trust companies in Brooklyn and thirty-eight in Manhattan. The table shows that New York City banks held approximately 85 percent of the total deposits of all trust companies in New York state, 90 percent of the cash reserves, and 88 percent of total reserves. With these proportions in mind we can examine the changes in select balance sheet items for all New York trusts between August 27 and December 10. The severe impact of the panic is evident from the 33 percent decline in total deposits, the 43 percent decrease in loans, and a 20 percent decline in cash reserves. Total resources contracted by $362 million. We can surmise that most of the contraction was in New York City. What is indeed surprising is that only one trust company in New York City permanently discontinued operations; the other reopened within a short period of time, indicative of the fact that the trust companies that succumbed were probably solvent at the time of closure. The severity of the impact can also be attributed to Morgan's initiatives that managed to keep the trust companies open, resulting in a sharp contraction of their loans and deposits and a massive injection of cash. The trust companies did not suspend cash payment; they agreed to pay depositors in certified checks on clearing house banks (Sprague, 1910, p. 258) to whatever extent possible.

Real Effects of the 1907 Panic

The financial and purely monetary effects of banking panics have received the most attention in the panic literature. Less attention, however, has been paid to the real effects; that is, to output and employment. For good reason: GNP and unemployment statistics were not available. Moreover, linking the banking panics to subsequent output and employment losses is not so simple. The panic may have sparked a recession in economic activity or a downturn may have preceded the panic. Recessions have a momentum of their own, and it would exaggerate the effects of the panic to assign to it all of the loss in output. How much of the output loss to assign to the banking panic per se is still an unresolved problem for all of the panics of the National banking era.

We are fortunate in having real GNP estimates for the pre- and post-panic years, but they are annual estimates. Quarterly estimates would, of course, be preferable and enable us to do a better job of identifying output effects, if any, that accompanied the banking panic. What do the real GNP estimates tell us? They do not speak with one voice. Both Romer (1989) and Balke-Gordon (1989) have prepared separate estimates, which are given below (in millions of dollars):

	Romer	Balke-Gordon
1906	351.5	367.7
1907	361.9	362.0
1908	346.8	342.2
1909	368.9	382.1

The two estimates almost exactly coincide for the panic year 1907 but there is no agreement about whether GNP increased by 3 percent, whereas Balke-Gordon show a 1.6 percent decline. Both indicate a decrease in real GNP in 1908. Romer's estimate of a 4.2 percent decrease is slightly lower than the Balke-Gordon estimate of 5.5 percent. Nevertheless, the 6.9 percent decline between 1906 and 1908 revealed by Balke-Gordon is much steeper than the 4.2 percent of Romer. The banking panic of 1907 was followed by a serious recession, more serious than the 5.7 percent decrease during the 1893 panic. This compares with increases in real GNP in 1873, 1884, and 1890, the single exception being the Balke-Gordon estimate of a 0.6 percent decline in 1873.

We may obtain some idea of the magnitude of the real effects of the 1907 panic by looking at bank clearings outside New York which were

Table 5.11. *Bank clearings outside New York,*
monthly, 1902, 1906, 1907 (in millions of dollars)

	1902	1906	1907
September	4,418	4,099	3,300
October	5,413	5,069	3,799
November	4,067	4,921	3,495
December	3,974	4,956	3,668

Source: *Bradstreet's*, December 7, 1907, p. 770, and
January 4, 1908, p. 3.

available monthly. Bank clearings outside New York were a good proxy
for GNP during the 1930s (Schwartz, 1981). Whether they were equally
reliable twenty years earlier, we do not know. But for what they are
worth, monthly estimates for September to December for 1902 and
1906–7 are shown in Table 5.11. By comparing bank clearings in a given
month with same month a year earlier, we can avoid the problem of not
having seasonally adjusted data.

No adverse effects of bank clearings in the panic month of October
are observable; in fact, bank clearings increased. The full impact,
however, fell in November and December. November clearings declined
17 percent from a year earlier, and 20 percent in December compared
with December 1906. *Bradstreet's* (January 4, 1908, p. 23) described business conditions in November as follows:

In November trade was at a low ebb, wholesale business was cut off, domestic
exchanges were distorted, collections fell to a very low value, cancellations were
numerous, industry was curtailed, forces and labor were reduced and wages cut
because of lack of money to meet payrolls.

The decline in bank clearings outside New York during the last three
months of 1907 compared with the final quarter of 1906 was greater than
the decline in bank clearings in the first quarter of 1908 compared with
the corresponding quarter one year before. The output effects in the
post-panic months were not negligible and are clearly consistent with the
output estimate of Balke-Gordon for 1907.

Table 5.12 shows the Lebergott and Romer's annual estimates of
unemployment from 1890 to 1910. Both reveal that the unemployment
rate increased in 1907; about one percentage point in Lebergott's estimate, somewhat less in Romer's. The unemployment rate increased to 8
percent in Lebergott and 6 percent in Romer, considerably less than the

Table 5.12. *Lebergott and Romer's annual estimates of the unemployment percentage, 1890–1910*

	Lebergott	Romer
1890	3.97	3.97
1891	5.42	4.77
1892	3.04	3.72
1893	11.68	8.09
1894	18.41	12.33
1895	13.70	11.11
1896	14.45	11.96
1897	14.54	12.43
1898	12.35	11.62
1899	6.54	8.66
1900	5.00	5.00
1901	4.13	4.59
1902	3.67	4.30
1903	3.92	4.35
1904	5.38	5.08
1905	4.28	4.62
1906	1.73	3.29
1907	2.76	3.57
1908	7.96	6.17
1909	5.11	5.13
1910	5.86	5.86

Source: Romer, 1986, p. 31.

18 percent rate (Lebergott) and the 12 percent rate (Romer) in the post-panic year of 1894. It is indeed puzzling why real GNP fell by more in 1907 than in 1893–94; the unemployment percentage was twice as high in the earlier panic.

Payroll difficulties which had played such an important roll in previous panics were muted, though not eliminated, by the innovative use of money substitutes (scrip) and the use by clearing houses in the interior of small-denominational certificates that were used to purchase goods and services. A Piatt Andrew (1908) estimated that 23 million dollars' worth of small denominational certificates were issued and 47 million dollars' worth of manufacturer's pay checks. The actual amounts were probably much greater.

Institutional Failure

Sprague (1910, p. 254) attributed the seriousness of the 1907 panic to what we now call institutional failure. The inference cannot be escaped that the "New York money market was not adequately organized to cope quickly and effectively with an emergency of this kind." Even with all of the benefits of hindsight, no more astute observation could be made today.

As we attempted to show, the NYCH had no difficulty in responding successfully to the first stage of the banking crisis. The NYCH provided direct financial support to at least two of the eight troubled banks associated with the Heinze, Morse, Thomas Brothers banking interests and went even further by demanding that each of the men withdraw from all association with banks receiving NYCH support. The Clearing House was also successful in keeping six of the eight banks open; two were forced to close. There was no general loss of depositor confidence in either New York or the interior. The NYCH had responded quickly and effectively to the banking disturbance.

It was the second stage that revealed a serious gap in the organization of the New York money market. The onset of a panic among the trust companies quickly demonstrated an organizational vacuum. There was no obvious place for them to turn for assistance. Since trust companies were not associated with NYCH, they could not expect support from that quarter. Moreover, the relationship between the trust companies and the clearing house banks had been strained by the intense rivalry for deposits, and the fact that they were not subject to the onerous regulation of reserve requirements.

The growth of the trust companies had been so rapid that insufficient attention had been paid to their growth as an additional potential source of banking instability. Nor had there been time to establish either a formal or informal organization of trust company officials to share mutual concerns. Nowhere was this more obvious than on the occasion when Morgan assembled the trust company presidents, as Satterlee reported that they had to be introduced to one another.

Needless to say, without the Morgan initiatives, trust company mutual support would not have been forthcoming. It may not have been necessary had the NYCH acted with greater dispatch in authorizing the issue of loan certificates. Under the circumstances, Sprague (1910, p. 252) thought the Knickerbocker suspension was unavoidable "in the absence of any association among the trust companies or any feeling of responsibility on the part of the clearing house banks." Had Knickerbocker not been a trust company, there can be little doubt, as we have stated before, in following the precedent established in 1884 of bank-specific intervention to keep it open.

The Morgan initiatives had at least one serious drawback: The separate responsibilities of the NYCH tended to become blurred by Morgan's strong leadership. Morgan attempted to muster the support of both the leaders of the largest clearing house banks and the trust company presidents. Both were usually present at the meetings convened by Morgan. The NYCH slipped into a merely passive role. That was unfortunate. Too much attention was directed at keeping the Trust Company of America and Lincoln Trust open in the face of persistent runs while insufficient attention was being paid to what was happening in the rest of the country.

Summary and Conclusions

The banking panic of 1907 was the most severe of the national banking era panics, not if measured by the number of bank suspensions, for they were few, but by deposits in failed banks – of which the Knickerbocker was by far the largest. Bank runs were more persistent than in the pre-panic week, lasting as long as three weeks in the case of the Trust Company America and the Lincoln Trust. The persistence can be attributed to what Sprague (1910, p. 257) referred to as the "cumbrous device of money pools." The money pools organized by Morgan did not forestall bank runs, though they did prevent the two largest trust companies from failing. Morgan's creditability did not rival that of the NYCH. His most serious error of judgment was the failure to provide aid to the Knickerbocker Trust. He had made up his mind from the beginning that the Knickerbocker did not deserve support because of its association with the Heinze-Morse speculations. Benjamin Strong, whose committee was responsible for determining Knickerbocker's solvency, never had the time to examine adequately the firm's assets. At worse the Knickerbocker was a case of borderline solvency as evidenced by the early resumption of normal operations in March 1908. Failure to support Knickerbocker destroyed depositor confidence in the other trust companies, who had no assurance that they would be bailed out.

Although Morgan's initiatives were not without fault, the behavior of the NYCH left much to be desired. Had the Clearing House responded immediately to the onset of the trust company panic by authorizing the issue of loan certificates without waiting three days, the money pooling arrangement of Morgan would probably have been unnecessary. Its negligence was further compounded by the decision to suspend cash payments. Neither total reserves nor their distribution called for suspension.

As indeed in previous panics the decision to suspend cash payments brought an increase in hoarding; there was a disruption of the domestic exchanges and an increase in the real costs of making transactions.

The panic spread to the interior when the country banks panicked and withdrew their balances from New York. Instead of expanding loans, they increased their holdings of excess reserves. Bank suspensions, nevertheless, were negligible in the interior.

The U.S. Treasury played a decisive role in implementing Morgan's money pool plans by depositing cash mainly in three New York national banks; this was the source of cash from which the trust companies could continue to pay out currency. Gold imports, though large, did little to increase the reserves of the New York banks.

We agree with Sprague that the fundamental cause of the panic was institutional failure – the failure of the NYCH to recognize any responsibility for maintaining banking stability in the New York money market, its failure to have authorized the issue of clearing house loan certificates quickly, its premature suspension of cash payments, and its unnecessary delay in the resumption of cash payment. The NYCH was quick to recognize its error in deciding not to aid the Knickerbocker Trust; it immediately initiated a change in policy to admit trust companies as members of the NYCH.

It is granted that J. P. Morgan filled a leadership vacuum by the reluctance of the NYCH to act decisively. We have attempted to show, however, that the Morgan initiatives were second best and had very little to teach us about how to avoid such a debacle in the future. "Ad hockery" had temporarily replaced wisdom accumulated in the four previous panics of the national banking era.

6 Were Panics of the National Banking Era Preventable?

In previous chapters our purpose has been to remove an information deficit about what happened both in New York and in the interior during the five banking disturbances of the national banking era. We learned that in two of the five, 1884 and 1890, the New York Clearing House responded quickly and effectively to ward off the spread of banking unrest to the interior. Cash payment was not suspended, and the number of bank runs and bank failures was negligible. However, during the banking panics of 1873, 1893, and 1907 the response of the NYCH left much to be desired, and the question naturally arises: If the Clearing House had done more, could the panics have been avoided? Surprising as it might seem, few attempts have been made to answer this question. And the reason why is that too little attention has been focused on the behavior of the NYCH and too much on the structural defects of the national banking system in conjunction with the normal seasonal flows of funds at crop moving time. According to the conventional wisdom, an inelastic stock of paper currency coupled with the pyramiding of the nations' ultimate banking reserve in New York made the central money market especially vulnerable to external shocks during the time crops were being harvested and shipped to the eastern seaboard. Little or no blame has been placed on the performance of the NYCH. Presumably the remedy did not reside in changing the behavior of the NYCH. What was needed was fundamental banking reform, notably the creation of a Federal Reserve System with the power to create a flexible note issue and a mechanism for increasing the stock of reserves in emergencies. At least one contemporary disagreed with the conventional wisdom. Sprague (1910) concluded that banking panics were not the consequence of a flawed banking system, flawed though it was. He argued that the NYCH lacked neither the knowledge nor the instruments to forestall banking panics. There was ample recognition of its responsibility as trustee of the ultimate banking reserve, though the acuteness of that per-

ception differed among the member banks. The NYCH had the power
to authorize the issue of loan certificates, to pool reserves, and to prohibit the payment of interest on bankers' balances. There was no disagreement about the perversity of a system that made no provision for
the suspension of reserve requirements during emergencies and no disagreement about the necessity for legislative relief.

To get the NYCH to act on that knowledge required leadership of a
high order. Dissident voices within the Clearing House posed a constant
threat to purposive action. Executive leadership was exercised by a president and a small executive committee. It would not be surprising that if
a strong and effective leader emerged, it was more by accident than by
design. Enforcement was not a problem since exclusion from the Clearing House was the ultimate penalty. When the leadership of the Clearing House was strong, as indeed it was in 1873, the Clearing House
behaved commendably though the suspension of cash payment was
not avoided. When the leadership was weak, the Clearing House pro-
crastinated by delaying the issue of clearing house loan certificates or
by failing to sanction the equalization of reserves. On these occasions
the individual banks apparently were more concerned with strengthen-
ing their own reserve position even if it was at the expense of their
associates.

There were devices available to the NYCH short of establishing a
central bank that could have prevented pre-1914 banking panics. But
their use required a resolute and persuasive leadership to surmount a
natural tendency of the member banks to give rent-seeking a higher pri-
ority than the pursuit of the public interest. We reexamine the Sprague
hypothesis and the evidence to support it.

The sole purpose of this chapter is to demonstrate the viability of the
NYCH control instruments and certain legislative changes in reserve
requirements to forestall banking panics. It is not intended as an argu-
ment against the creation of the Federal Reserve System. Nor does it
address the question of whether a central bank would be a more effective mechanism for preventing banking panics, though my personal preference is for a central bank rather than a voluntary association of private
bankers.

The first section describes the behavior of total reserves of the NYCH
banks during pre-1914 banking panics and emphasizes the significance
of the concentration of the banking reserve in New York. The two principal instruments of Clearing House policy – loan certificates and reserve
pooling – are analyzed in the second section. The third section explains
how reserve availability was constrained by the existence of fixed
reserve/deposit ratios. A Clearing House plan to prevent banking panics

– the Coe Report – is summarized in the fourth section. The fifth section describes briefly Sprague's two specifics of NYCH behavior for preventing banking panics. The role of gold imports and U.S. Treasury assistance in moderating the panics of the national banking era are analyzed in the sixth section. The seventh section provides alternative explanations of why the NYCH failed to authorize reserve pooling in the post-1873 panics. An epilogue concludes the chapter.

The Behavior of Reserves of the NYCH Banks

The key to understanding what happened during banking panics of the national banking era is the behavior of the reserves of the NYCH banks, the chief characteristics of which were their size, distribution, and volatility. It was the threat, either real or alleged, to the reserve position of the NYCH banks that explains the Clearing House response in issuing clearing house loan certificates and suspending cash payments.

The concentration of the banking reserve in New York increased the vulnerability of the central money market to financial shocks. The withdrawal of bankers' balances of the interior banks eroded the reserves of the NYCH banks, thereby increasing the risk of the suspension of cash payments.

The explanation for the concentration of the banking reserve in New York includes both financial and nonfinancial considerations. Of the financial determinants two have received the most attention: reserve pyramiding sanctioned by the National Banking Act and the payment of interest on balances held by interior banks. National banks were required to hold a fixed and invariant ratio of reserves (specie plus legal tender currency) to deposit liabilities. The size of that ratio was determined by a three-tier bank classification scheme. The required reserve ratio for central reserve city banks (New York and later Chicago and St. Louis) was 25 percent to be held in cash in their own vaults; for reserve city banks it was also 25 percent, half of which could be held on deposit in central reserve city banks. For all the remaining banks which were labeled country banks the ratio was 15 percent, 60 percent of which could be held as deposits in either central reserve or reserve city banks. Pyramiding, however, did not explain why reserve city and country banks decided to place both surplus reserve as well as required reserves in New York. There had to be a strong monetary incentive in the form of interest payments on bankers' balances.

Myers (1931, p. 103) attributed the concentration of the banking reserve in New York to interregional flows-of-trade considerations, a process that had begun well before the passage of the National Banking

Act. The continuous flow of deposits to New York was the result of the city's importance as an emporium for trade with the interior. Interior banks recognized early on that balances held in New York yielded greater benefits than balances held at home. For example, the rate of domestic exchange was generally in favor of New York, and commercial paper bearing New York names was more desirable than that of local merchants. New York balances were also desirable by interior banks as the designated place of note redemption.

Myers also maintained that the payment of interest on bankers' balances had less to do with the inflow of funds to New York than in determining which New York banks reaped the benefits of the inflow. Neither reserve pyramiding nor interest payments on bankers' balances explain by themselves the concentration of the banking reserve in New York. But what is still lacking is any effort to quantify the individual factors that were responsible for reserve concentration and for what particular periods.

Not only were banking reserves concentrated in New York but they were concentrated among a few banks. Of the approximately sixty members of the NYCH at least fifteen held almost all of the banker's balances of the New York banks. According to Sprague (1910, p. 233) seven of these banks in 1873 controlled 30 percent of all the resources of the New York banks, one-third of the loans, and two-fifths of the cash reserve. By 1907 the degree of concentration of total reserves, loans, and cash reserves had increased substantially. Six banks holding the core of bankers' deposits controlled over 60 percent of the total resources of the New York banks, 60 percent of the loans, and two-thirds of the cash reserves. Sprague concluded (1910, p. 234), perhaps surprisingly, that they "would have yielded a banking power sufficient, it may be readily believed, for almost any emergency." However, he failed to explain how these various indices of "banking power" were related to specific panic-prevention measures. If banking power was sufficient for almost any emergency, it would seem to suggest that there must have been serious problems in harnessing that power to achieve the goal of panic prevention. As we shall see, he pointed repeatedly to the problems raised by the distribution of reserves between the six or seven banks and the rest of the banks in New York, and the problems raised by the unwillingness of all the New York banks to use their reserves freely in emergencies, except, perhaps in 1873. The avoidance of suspension was quite simply a matter of the New York banks having an adequate reserve and for that reserve to have been distributed fairly evenly among the larger banks. The issue of clearing house loan certificates eliminated the need for currency to settle local interbank indebtedness.

Table 6.1. *Behavior of total reserves of New York banks, weekly, beginning with the first panic week (in millions of dollars)*

Week	1873	1884	1890	1893 May	June	July–August	1907
1	57.1	84.1	95.5	121.4	134.7	94.3	254.7*
2	53.1	86.9	95.8	126.5	128.9	96.4	224.1
3	34.1*	82.4	95.5	134.1	119.7	91.2	219.8
4	22.6	67.5	95.0	134.7	119.1*	79.2	218.7
5	22.1	70.1			105.0	76.5	215.9
6	19.7					80.5	217.8

Source: Sprague, 1910.
*Suspension of cash payment.

Now we turn to the behavior of the banking reserve in New York during each of the five banking disturbances of the national banking era. The behavior of total and surplus reserves weekly beginning with the first panic week of the NYCH banks is set out in Tables 6.1 and 6.2. What Table 6.1 reveals is that at no time was there ever any real threat to the average reserve position of the NYCH banks, with the possible exception of 1873. The level of total reserves remained relatively high in 1884, 1890, 1893, and 1907, and it did not act as a serious constraint to the continuation of cash payments. If reserves had been equalized in 1893 and 1907, as they had been in 1873, suspension might easily have been avoided. The explanation why equalization failed to prevent suspension of cash payment in 1873 is postponed until we have discussed more fully reserve equalization as an instrument for preventing banking panics.

It is clear from Table 6.1 that Clearing House bank reserve behavior in 1873 differed from that in subsequent panics. Even after the suspension of cash payments in 1873, the banks continued to pay out currency freely in a manner that Walter Bagehot would have applauded, that is, the continuation of cash payment to the point of a near-exhaustion of bank reserves!

Except for the week following suspension there was little or no change in total reserves during subsequent banking panics. The 1873 Clearing House policy of freely paying out currency after suspension had been abandoned in the panics of 1893 and 1907. The refusal of the Clearing House to equalize reserves in 1893 made suspension unavoidable after a few of the larger interest-paying banks had depleted their reserves. In

Table 6.2. *Surplus reserves of New York banks,*
weekly, beginning with first panic week

Week	1873	1884	1890	1893 (July/Aug.)	1907
1	−1.5	0.8	−2.6	−4.3	−1.0
2	−3.2	4.5	−0.8	−1.3	−38.8
3	−9.5*	3.1	0.1	−4.3	−51.9
4	−16.5	−6.6	0.4	−14.0	−53.7
5	−16.9	−2.0	−2.4	−16.5	−54.1
6	−18.8	1.3	0.6	−12.1	−53.0
7	−15.5	7.0		−6.7	−46.2
8	−9.0	10.0		−1.6	−40.1
9	−1.6			+3.0	−31.8
10	+2.2				−20.2
11	+12.0				−11.5
12					+6.1

Source: Weekly bank statements published in *New York Times*.

*No surplus reserves figures were published after the second panic week. In 1875, Clearing House data were published in *Bankers' Magazine* (p. 829). I derived surplus reserves by taking total deposits ×0.25 (reg. res. ratio) = required reserves; I subtracted required reserves from total reserves to obtain an estimate of surplus reserves.

1907 the size of the reserves was adequate but its distribution was uneven among the banks.

The fact that reserves barely changed in 1890 (less than 1 percent) should inject serious doubt about the existence of a general banking panic. Neither the banking disturbance of 1884 nor 1890 reveals a sequence of reserve deficits (Table 6.2) comparable with the other three panics, but, of course, we know that there was no suspension of cash payment; the loss of confidence did not reach the interior banks.

The 1893 panic was unique in both duration and the unusually large number of bank suspensions throughout the country. May, June, July, and August have been labeled panic months. But the evidence of a banking panic is not observable in either total reserves or surplus reserves in the month of May. Total reserves increased 11 percent and surplus reserves nearly doubled. In June total reserves declined by $30 million (22%) and surplus reserves decreased by $25 million to a mere $6 million, though still remaining positive. Bank suspensions accelerated in July; total reserves decreased by only $3 million and a reserve deficit emerged for the first time and remained substantial for the next ten weeks. Reserve deficits were recorded during the first panic week in 1873, 1890, 1893, and 1907. The existence of a reserve deficit coincided with the duration of suspension: a little over one month in 1873, one month in 1893, and two months in 1907.

In sum the concentration of the country's banking reserve in New York increased the susceptibility of the New York banks to withdrawals of the highly volatile balances of the interior banks. At the slightest signal of banking unrest in the central money market, the interior banks withdrew their balances, thereby contracting the reserves of the New York banks and posing the immediate threat of a suspension of cash payment. The effects of increased demands for currency in the interior, whether due to normal seasonal demands or to loss of depositor or bankers' confidence, could be satisfied only from the inelastic stock of reserves of the New York banks. It was the volatility of an inelastic stock of reserves concentrated in the central money market that made the New York banks especially vulnerable to shocks to banker or depositor confidence. The average level of reserves of the NYCH banks was never a threat to cash payment, except perhaps in 1873. As we see below, it was the distribution of the banking reserve among the member banks that prompted suspension.

Instruments of Clearing House Policy

The New York Clearing House had at its disposal two powerful instruments with which to forestall banking panics. It could authorize the issue of clearing house loan certificates by the member banks, which, in fact, it voted to do in each of the five banking disturbances of the pre-1914 era. It could also pool (equalize) their reserves, which it approved only on the occasion of the 1873 panic.

The clearing house loan certificate was a device to conserve the currency reserves of the NYCH banks without impairing their capacity to expand loans locally. For all intents and purposes loan certificates were quasi-reserves since they served as a means of payment at the Clearing House. The amount of certificates issued depended on the discretion of a clearing house committee and the willingness of the debtor banks to pay 7 percent interest. The rate was set sufficiently high to insure their retirement at the end of the crisis. According to Sprague (1910, p. 49) it removed the temptation of a single bank to strengthen itself at the other's expense. Moreover, by making provision of settling Clearing

Table 6.3. *Dates, duration, and amount of NYCH loan certificate issues in five banking disturbances*

Date of first issue	Duration of issue (days)	Amount issued (millions of dollars)	Reserves of NYC banks*	Ratio of total certificates issued to reserves
1873 Sept. 22	59	22.4	57.1	39.2
1884 May 15	21	21.9	N.A.	N.A.
1890 Nov. 12	40	15.2	95.8	15.9
1893 June 21	77	38.2	135.0	28.3
1907 Oct. 26	95	101.1	167.0	37.8

Source: Sprague, 1910, p. 433.
*Reserve data: September 13, 1873; November 15, 1890; May 27, 1893; and October 19, 1907.

House deficits the New York banks could expand loans to their local clients, in particular to absorb call loans liquidated by interior banks. Banks were expected to continue to pay out currency freely to the nonbank public.

The assurance of Clearing House support was supposed to restore confidence in the solvency of the NYCH banks and serve as a deterrent to withdrawals by interior banks. The number of bank suspensions and bank runs in New York was negligible after the issue of loan certificates. The loan certificates were successful in ending bank suspensions in New York.

Most of the evidence, though not all, in Table 6.3 confirms what we already know about the relative severity of the five banking panics as measured by either the number of bank suspensions or deposits in suspended banks. The 1884 and 1890 panics were the mildest; in neither panic did the NYCH suspend cash payments. Only $15.2 million of loan certificates were issued in 1890, far less than the amounts issued in the other four panics. The duration of the certificates issued was barely five weeks. Duration is an index of the seriousness of each banking crisis, the assumption being the shorter the period during which loan certificates were issued, the milder the panic. However, that may not always be the case. The NYCH banks may have been less inclined to take out certificates in some panic episodes than in others (Sprague, 1910, p. 215).

In 1884, the duration was barely three weeks, though the amount of loan certificates was only slightly less than in 1873. The 1893 and 1907 panics were the most severe; there were more bank suspensions in 1893

Table 6.4. *Loan certificates issued and total deposits of NYCH for each of the banking disturbances, 1873–1907*

	Deposits	Loan certificates	Loan certificates as a percent of deposits
1873	152,640,000	22,410,000	14.7
1884	296,575,300	21,885,000	7.3
1890	376,746,500	15,205,000	4.0
1893	374,000,000	38,280,000	10.2
1907*	824,400,000	10,000,000	12.3

Source: NYCH Committee Minutes, pp. 160–165, November 2, 1893.
*For 1907: Minutes of the Subcommittee Associate Bank Officers Appointed October 16, 1907.

and a larger amount of deposits in suspended banks in 1907. Evidence in Table 6.3 reveals that the 1907 panic ranks first in both the amount of loan certificates issued ($101 million) – two and a half times more than in the 1873 panic and 4.6 times more than in 1890 – and the length of the period during which loan certificates were issued (13 weeks). The 1893 panic ranks midway between the relatively mild 1884 and 1890 panics and the more severe 1893 and 1907 panics. Cash payments were suspended in the latter two.

Since loan certificate issue represents a temporary increase in the reserve of the NYCH banks for a specific purpose – the discharge of clearing house indebtedness – a better measure of the significance of the increase may be the ratio of total loan certificates issued to the amount of NYCH reserves on the date nearest to the time when the first certificates were issued. These ratios are shown in the last column of Table 6.3. The 1890 panic shows the lowest ratio, but the 1873 panic has a slightly higher ratio than that of 1907, although the absolute level of loan certificates was only one-fifth of the 1907 issues.

An alternate measure of the relative significance of the issue of loan certificates is given in Table 6.4 for each of the five banking disturbances of the National Banking Era: the ratio of loan certificates issued to deposits in NYCH banks. Loan certificates as a percentage of deposits was greater in 1873, much higher than in 1893 and 1907 when the panics were more severe; it was negligible in 1890.

Did the issue of loan certificates prevent loan contraction by the NYCH banks? Data in Table 6.5 shows loan contraction by NYCH banks

Table 6.5. *Change in loans of NYCH banks, weekly, beginning with week loan certificates were issued in each of the five panics*

	1873	1884	1890	1893		1907
				July 17–July 18	July 22–Aug. 5	
1	−6	−6.8	−5.6	−5	−4.3	+10
2	−12	−13.4	−6.0		−2.7	+60.7
3	2	−3.6	−2.8	+13	+2.2	+38.9
4	−3	−7.0	+2.0	−5		
5	−4	−6.7	−0.5			
6	−7	−2.8	+0.4			
7	−1					
8	−4					

Source: Sprague, 1910.

in 1873, 1884, 1890, and the second panic month in 1893. Loans expanded during the first panic month in 1893 and during 1907. What is immediately apparent is the strong loan expansion in 1907. During the first three weeks beginning with the week loan certificates were issued, loans increased by $110 million. Loan data for each of the six most important clearing house banks between October 19 and 26 reveal that all but two of the banks increased their loans; the increase was greatest in only two of the six. Sprague (1910, p. 268) did not think that these two banks were doing their utmost to relieve the situation. However, that did not prevent him from concluding that the loan response in 1907 was "eminently wise and proper and in accord with the requirements of the situation." It is also clear that reserve deficits which were especially large were not a hindrance to further loan expansion.

In 1884 and 1890 the issue of loan certificates was adequate to allay the panic. Cash payments were not suspended in either New York or the interior; bank suspensions were negligible and the duration of the panics was brief.

The issue of loan certificates, however, was no guarantee the interior banks would refrain from withdrawing sizable amounts of currency from the NYCH banks. And all of the clearing house banks were not affected equally by the currency demands of the interior banks; the burden of the drain had to be absorbed by the handful of interest-paying banks that held the bulk of the bankers' balances, and of these some were better endowed with cash than others. To prevent suspension of payment by cash-deficient banks, a means had to be devised to transfer funds from banks with surplus cash to banks with a cash deficiency. If the currency reserves of the NYCH banks were pooled, they could be redistributed in accord with need, thereby forestalling the suspension of cash payments.

This pooling arrangement was referred to as the equalization of reserves, whereby the Clearing House assumed control over the reserves of the member banks. It had been used on two previous occasions in 1860 and 1861 (NYCH Association, Minutes, Nov. 21, 1860, and April 25, 1861). Sprague thought (1910, p. 90) that this pooling arrangement made the resources of the NYCH banks greater than that of any European central bank! A resolution adopted by the New York Clearing House on Saturday evening, September 20, 1873, included the following:

That, in order to accomplish the purposes set forth in this arrangement, the legal tenders belonging to the associated banks shall be considered and treated as a common fund, held for mutual aid and protection, and the committee appointed shall have the power to equalize the same by assessment, or otherwise at their discretion.

For this purpose a statement shall be made to the committee on the condition of each bank on the morning of every day, before the commencement of business, which shall be sent with exchanges to the manager of the clearing house, specifying the following items:

  1st – amount of loans and discounts;
  2nd – amount of loan certificates;
  3rd – amount of United States certificates of deposit and legal tender notes; and,
  4th – amount of deposits, deducting therefrom the amount of special gold deposits.

Reserves were equalized in 1873 but in no other panic of the national banking era. To Sprague that was regrettable, for the suspension of cash payment in both 1893 and 1907 resulted solely from an unequal distribution of reserves among the large money center banks holding most of the bankers' balances. He conjectured (1910, p. 183) that if reserves had been equalized in 1893 it was "highly probable, indeed, a practical certainty that suspension would not have been necessary," and in 1907 (Sprague, 1910, p. 273) "it can be questioned for a moment that suspension would not have occurred had similar action been taken in 1907 nor would agreement by all clearing-house members have been necessary." Friedman and Schwartz (1963, p. 160) also concluded that equalization of reserves would have prevented suspension in 1907: "An attempt to maintain payments by pooling reserves and satisfying the country banks'

Table 6.6. *Legal tender currency of New York banks, weekly September–October 1873*

		Level (millions of dollars)	Change
September	20	34.2	
	27	21.2	−13
October	4	12	−9.2
	11	10.2	−1.8
	18	6.3	−3.9
	25	8.8	2.5
November	1	14.7	5.9
	8	21	6.3

Source: Sprague, 1910, p. 55.

demand for currency might have ended the demands promptly without seriously reducing reserves."

Why, then, did reserve equalization fail to prevent the suspension of cash payments in 1873? It was Sprague's considered judgment that the New York banks held an inadequate level of reserves immediately prior to the panic. Table 6.1 shows that the clearing house banks held $53 million of reserves prior to suspension. The NYCH banks partially suspended cash payment on September 24. The balance sheet of the New York banks for the week ending September 26 showed a decrease in legal tender currency of $13 million from the preceding week, or a 38 percent decrease. The proportion of reserves to deposits had fallen from 23 to 16.97 percent. Sprague concluded: "the banks were clearly at the end of their resources, and the step taken on Wednesday, September 24 seems amply justified" (p. 54).

The weekly level and change for September 20 to November 8 in legal tender currency of the New York banks are given in Table 6.6. Specie is omitted because it did not circulate. What is clear is that the New York banks continued to pay out currency to interior banks almost as freely as before suspension, mainly as a result of the equalization of reserves. By October 18 reserves had fallen to $6.3 million; the reserve deficit reached $25.6 million. The New York banks had done all within their power to maintain cash payment to interior banks by ignoring the reserve ratio constraint.

Can we conclude from this experience that the suspension of cash payment might have been avoided, given the New York banks' willingness to pay out currency freely until it was almost gone? Although Bagehot's *Lombard Street* was published in 1873, the New York banks were acting as though they were following his precepts, that is, lend freely and continue to pay out currency!

What we do know from pre-1914 bank panic experience is that an increase in hoarding always accompanied the suspension of cash payment. The figures on the behavior of legal tender holdings of the NYCH banks reflects post-suspension experience; they say nothing about what would have happened if cash payments had not been suspended. The equalization of reserves alone would have dispelled the doubts of interior bankers about the ability of the Clearing House to maintain the liquidity and solvency of the New York banks. The restoration of confidence in the New York banks would have eliminated any incentive to withdraw bankers' balances.

It is to be noted that knowledge about what happened to hoarding after the suspension of cash payments to agents in 1873 did not become available until much later. We do not disagree with Sprague's judgment that the Clearing House was probably justified, on the basis of the knowledge available at the time, to suspend in 1873. But there was no real economic necessity to do so. Equalization of reserves was an effective remedy for mobilizing the reserves of the New York banks in the absence of a central bank with the power to create reserves.

Reserve Availability and Fixed Reserve/Deposit Ratios

The American system of banking placed a legal obstacle in the path of reserve availability in times of financial emergencies. The fixed reserve requirement antedated the National Banking Act and was originally designed to insure bank liquidity. However, no provision was made to suspend or reduce the reserve requirement in time of crisis. National banks were not legally permitted to lend when they experienced a reserve deficit, but they were not prohibited from paying out cash. There is no evidence that the Comptroller of the Currency attempted to enforce sanctions when national banks suffered reserve deficits. In fact, the Comptroller actively encouraged lending during panic periods.

Financial markets, nevertheless, monitored closely the behavior of at least three measures of reserve availability: (1) the actual reserve ratio in relation to the legal ratio of 25 percent, (2) surplus reserves (total reserves minus required reserves), and (3) the reserve deficit (the negative of surplus reserves). All three were available weekly in the financial press and served as leading indicators of the state of the money market.

As such they provided a basis for the formation of expectations about the behavior of NYCH banks. For example, the emergence of a reserve deficit foreshadowed loan and deposit contraction by the New York banks as they attempted to eliminate the reserve deficit.

As Tables 6.2 and 6.5 show for all panics with the exception of 1907, loan contraction and the reserve deficit for NYCH banks moved together. It is also clear that the duration of the suspension of cash payments was determined primarily by how long it took to eliminate that deficit. The timing of the suspension of cash payment except in 1873 was dictated not by the state of total reserves but by the status of the reserve deficit, implicit recognition that when there was a reserve deficit, reserves were not available to meet the withdrawal demands of the interior banks.

It still remains a puzzle how the device of legal reserve requirements which was originally introduced to provide liquidity in time of crisis became a key instrument for restricting liquidity! This anomalous situation did not go unnoticed by members of the NYCH. The Coe Report, a report of a special Clearing House committee in 1873, strongly denounced inflexible reserve requirements: "There seems an intrinsic absurdity in a law requiring that a 'reserve' must be always kept which was created on purpose to be used, or that a bank officer who draws upon the reserve, under circumstances for which it was intended, is false to the oath which he takes to obey the law." The committee thought that Congress should give the NYCH the authority to suspend or relax reserve requirements during emergencies. George Perkins (U.S. House of Representatives, p. 1612) repeated a story attributed to J. P. Morgan. One banker said to Morgan: "I am very much disturbed: I am below my legal reserve," and Morgan replied: "You ought to be ashamed of yourself to be anywhere near your legal reserve. What is your reserve for at a time like this except to use!"

The Coe Report: A Clearing House Plan to Prevent Panics

In November 1873, shortly after the end of the panic, a special committee of the NYCH issued a report that was acclaimed by Sprague (1910, p. 90) as "the ablest document which has ever appeared in the course of our banking history." The chairman of the committee was George S. Coe, president of the American Exchange Bank, who, if not the ablest banker in the United States at that time, was one of the ablest. Redlich (1968, pp. 424–38) in his brief biographical sketch attributed the origins of the Clearing House loan certificate to Coe. He may very well have

George Simmons Coe, Chairman of the New York Clearing
House Association.

been responsible for the reserve equalization scheme as well. Coe fervently believed that the NYCH banks possessed the power as well as the resources to prevent future banking panics "without resorting to any deliberately formal legal or corporate organization." A purely voluntary association of New York banks that recognized its responsibility for the maintenance of banking stability was a feasible solution to the bank panic problem. The Coe Report attempted to make the case that banking panics could be averted if the Clearing House exercised bold leadership and was fully prepared to use its power and instruments to achieve its objective. Sprague's unqualified praise will probably come as a surprise to students of U.S. banking history who are unfamiliar with the Coe Report or its contents. Because of its unfamiliarity and its importance I provide a detailed analysis of its contents.

In the absence of a central bank the responsibilities of the NYCH were sharply defined: "It must always be remembered that in the absence of any important central institution, such as exists in other commercial nations, the associated banks [of the Clearing House] are the last resort in this country, in times of financial extremity, and upon their stability and sound conduct the national prosperity greatly depends" (Sprague, 1910, p. 95). In a speech Coe delivered to the NYCH in June 1884, he made more explicit the central institution to which the 1873 report referred: "Like the Bank of England in the British financial system, the banks are the final reservoir of the cash reserve of nation and its refuge in commercial commotion" (Sprague, 1910, pp. 374–75). The 1873 report condemned any clearing house bank that presumed that its own interests were paramount: "No institution, therefore, has a moral right to conduct its affairs with the public in defiance of the general conviction of its associates, or to introduce private terms of dealing with its customers which are in the best interests of all" (Sprague, 1910, p. 95). No stronger statement was possible emanating from the NYCH about the collective responsibilities of the individual banks.

The report identified the main problem during panics as one of an insufficiency of reserves, to be remedied in the following ways. Perhaps the most effective device for guaranteeing the maximum use of reserves in emergencies was the power of the Clearing House to equalize reserves of member banks. The report stated:

An expedient was found by which the stronger banks placed themselves under the unequal burden and equalized the pressure of gathering in their resources and placing them at the disposal of the weaker, who were thus furnished with the means to meet the demands of their depositors and to save themselves from public exposure and their dealers in city and country from disaster and ruin. (Sprague, 1910, p. 94)

The NYCH should request authority from Congress to allow the Clearing House after consultation with the Treasury Secretary to relax reserve requirements, and it should also request authority from Congress to vary interest rates to protect the banking reserve. Such authority was necessary because of a legal constraint placed on the increase in rates by New York State usury laws.

The report also perceived correctly the proper use of the banking reserve as a fund held for specific use in emergencies. The report also stated: "The practical difficulty consists of attaching a rigid and inflexible rule of law to a mobile fund which is held for the purpose of meeting sudden emergencies, which is, therefore, in its very nature a variable quantity. It is impossible to prescribe by statute the circumstances or the exact priorities during which the reserve should be increased or decreased" (Sprague, 1910, p. 95).

To reduce the volatility of banker's deposits, the report also called for the cessation of interest payments on interior bank balances held in New York. Surplus reserves of the interior banks tended to accumulate in New York at periods of low seasonal demand attracted by the high rates available in New York. At the first sign of banking distress in New York, interior banks commenced to withdraw their balances which had mainly been employed as call loans to the stock market. The attempt to contract call loans put added pressure on brokerage firms, who in their scramble for alternative financing bid up call money rates. The remedy, according to the committee, was to cease the payment of interest on interbank balances, which should provide a strong incentive for interior banks to redistribute their reserves between cash and deposits with other banks. The effect presumably would strengthen the cash reserves of out-of-town banks and reduce their dependence on the New York money market.

The 1873 report was a tribute to Coe's leadership and demonstrated a remarkable grasp for the time of the responsibilities of the NYCH banks for preventing banking panics. One must concur with Sprague's perceptive judgment about the value of his report in U.S. banking history.

Sprague on the Treatment of Banking Panics

Sprague accepted the analysis and remedies for pre-1914 banking panics contained in the Coe Report. He enunciated "two specifics for the treatment of a panic": the continuance of loans to solvent borrowers, and "the prompt payment by the banks of every demand by depositors for cash" (1910, p. 144). The first could be expedited by the issue of clearing house loan certificates, and the second by the equalization of reserves. It is indeed curious that Sprague does not refer even once to Walter Bagehot's *Lombard Street*, published thirty-seven years before his *History of Crises*. Nevertheless, his "two specifics" for the treatment of a panic repeat Bagehot's famous principles (1887, pp. 173, 187):

1. "Theory suggests, and experience proves, that in a panic the holders of the ultimate bank reserve (whether one bank or many) should lend to all that bring good securities quickly, freely, and readily. By that policy they allay a panic; by every other policy they intensify it."
2. It is the duty of the Bank of England "not only to keep a good reserve effectively when that time of panic comes. The keepers of the Banking reserve, whether one or many, are obliged then to use that reserve for their own safety."

It is clear from the phrase "whether one bank or many" that Bagehot meant his two principles to apply either to one bank such as the Bank of England or to many banks holding the ultimate banking reserve of the country. Whether deliberate or not, Bagehot was addressing the banks of the NYCH as well.

I do not think that there can be any doubt that Sprague was well acquainted with *Lombard Street*, though I find it baffling why it is not mentioned in his *History of Crises*. He certainly inherited his strong distaste for the suspension of cash payments from him. Suspension was unthinkable to Bagehot. He acknowledged that reserves conceivably could be inadequate; however, he remained intrepid: "The only safe plan for the Bank is the brave plan, to lend in a panic on every kind of current security, or on every sort on which money is ordinarily and usually lent. This policy may not save the Bank; but if it does not, nothing will save it" (Bagehot, 1987, p. 199). According to Bagehot no constraints whatsoever should be placed on the paying out freely of the reserve.

Sprague, like Bagehot, considered suspension of cash payments as a policy to be avoided at all possible costs. His attempts to quantify the costs of suspension were necessarily crude. Nevertheless, his account of suspensions in 1873, 1893, and 1907 does chronicle the hardships associated with a lack of currency to meet payrolls, delays in the shipment of commodities, the discharge of workers, and the temporary closing of some plants and firms. Neither Sprague nor anyone else has been able to estimate the employment and output effects of suspension apart from the effects of the ensuing recession or depression.

Friedman and Schwartz (1963, p. 698) did not deny that suspension of cash payments was costly. But they considered suspension as less costly than the prospect of continued bank failures in its absence; for example, suspension in 1907 "was a therapeutic measure which cut short the liquidity crisis, prevented good banks from failing in droves as victims of mass hysteria and, at the cost of severe but brief difficulties, enabled recovery and expansion to come after a short-lived contraction." But they agreed fully with Sprague that the equalization of reserves, if it had been adopted in 1907, would have prevented suspension and a worsening of the panic (p. 160). Contrary to the attempts by Timberlake (1984, p. 11) and Dewald (1972, p. 937) to drive a wedge between Sprague and Friedman and Schwartz on whether suspension was a lesser evil than continued bank suspensions, both Sprague and Friedman and Schwartz viewed suspension as unavoidable if reserves were not equalized.

Supplementary Sources of Reserves: Gold Imports and U.S. Treasury Assistance

The national banking system contained no mechanism for increasing the stock of bank reserves during banking panics except the issue of loan certificates. There were, however, two external sources of relief in emergencies: gold imports and U.S. Treasury purchases of government securities and deposit transfers to commercial banks. Neither, however, could be relied upon to provide timely and adequate support to forestall banking panics. Preconditions were necessary to evoke such assistance. Gold imports were induced by a proper configuration of exchange rates, and Treasury support depended on the existence of a fiscal surplus. A currency premium coupled with an export surplus could move the exchange rate below the gold import point and thereby induce a gold inflow. Currency premia emerged after the suspension of cash payments in 1873, 1893, and 1907. Treasury assistance, especially before the 1907 panic, took the form of debt repayment: the purchase of U.S. government securities, the proceeds of which were deposited in the form of currency mainly in New York banks. If conditions were propitious, gold imports and Treasury purchases of securities could moderate the panic by hastening the end of suspension. We examine each in turn.

U.S. Treasury Assistance

During the pre-1914 period, outside assistance was frequently provided by the U.S. Treasury to prevent or moderate money market stringency where money market stringency did not always evolve into a full-scale banking panic. Treasury intervention took the form of government security purchases – bond redemption – financed out of an accumulated budget surplus; the prices paid by the Treasury for its securities could not exceed par in gold. After 1900, intervention occurred through changes in U.S. government deposits at commercial banks. Bond purchases per se did not necessarily supply the commercial banks with either reserves or currency; whether it did or not depended on from whom the bonds were purchased and the disposition of the proceeds.

The market interpreted the existence of surplus funds in the Treasury as indicative of its willingness to place funds at the disposal of the New York banks in an emergency, which quite possibly weakened their resolve to hold larger bank reserves. The Treasury on this view could be expected to provide support when and if needed. Sprague (1910, p. 231) doubted, however, the allegation that the Treasury could be expected to provide support on the grounds that the New York banks had always loaned to the full extent of their resources.

Except perhaps in 1890, relief provided by the U.S. Treasury did not change the course of the banking panic. In 1873, for example, the New York Subtreasury paid out $27 million on September 20, the peak panic day. Savings banks were the principal source of the sales, and they preferred to hold currency rather than deposit the proceeds in commercial banks. Sprague (1910, p. 42) concluded that Treasury bond purchases were of "slight service in relieving the situation." No Treasury assistance was offered in 1884, and in 1893 Treasury payments added only $9 million to currency in circulation in August, the final month of the panic and after payment had been suspended. During the 1907 panic the Treasury offered support in two forms: It issued 50 million dollars' worth of 2 percent Panama bonds for the purpose of encouraging the issuance of national bank notes, and the Treasury purchased $39 million in bonds in December for the explicit purpose of adding to the money stock. This action was probably unnecessary, since funds had already begun to flow back into the banks (Sprague, 1910, p. 317). In 1890, there was massive intervention by the Treasury for the explicit purpose of supplying funds to meet the autumnal crop needs. The Treasury redeemed $50 million of government bonds between August and September to alleviate monetary stringency. There were, however, no bank suspensions nor a banking disturbance before the second week in November. Once the disturbance erupted, the Treasury did not see the need for additional assistance.

The evidence suggests that the Treasury intervened selectively to provide assistance to an agitated money market. But intervention was less frequent and less effective after the panic was under way. We have to conclude with Sprague that Treasury assistance played a minor role in pre-1914 panics and was not a decisive factor in their termination.

Gold Imports

The supply of currency could also be augmented from external sources, chiefly gold imports. The ability to obtain gold in emergencies obviated money market stringency by increasing the reserves of the New York banks. But there was an inevitable delay of at least two weeks to allow for gold shipment time between the United States and Europe. Gold imports were a device for circumventing the fixity of the stock of paper money, both greenbacks and national bank notes.

The mechanism for inducing gold imports was the behavior of exchange rates. When exchange rates dipped below the gold import point, an incentive emerged to import gold. The emergence of a currency premium after the suspension of cash payments through its effect on the exchange rates was also thought to be an important cause of gold imports. However, Sprague (1910, p. 193) considered the currency premium to be only one influence and not the most important. Both exchange rates and the currency premium were affected in turn by the merchandise trade balance.

The behavior of gold imports during the pre-1914 banking panics does not reveal that these effects were very substantial. The role of gold imports in moderating banking panics was negligible in 1884 and 1890. And although between September 25 and the end of October 1873 some 15 million dollars' worth of gold was imported, the effect was minimal because the United States was on an inconvertible paper standard. Gold payments were not resumed before 1879. Although gold added to the reserves of the New York banks, domestic gold payments were negligible and contributed nothing to the restoration of their cash (legal tender) reserve.

During the 1907 panic, gold imports were enormous: $25 million during the week ending November 1, $58 million in November, and $38 million in December – over $100 million in two months. But no use was made of the incoming gold by the New York banks; no effort was made to end the suspension of cash payments. Suspension did not end until cash began to flow back from the interior.

In August 1893, the month when cash payment was suspended, 40 million dollars' worth of gold was imported and was responsible more than any other single factor for bringing an end to suspension. Gold imports amounted to only $5 million between the middle of June and the end of July and another $10 million during the first week of August.

Gold imports were not a decisive influence in moderating banking panics in the pre-1914 period, with possible exception of 1893 when it might have shortened the duration of suspension. But that was not the case in 1907. Gold inflows were not part of an automatic response mechanism to banking panics.

Apologia for Clearing House Bank Inaction

As we attempted to show by the extended analysis of the Coe Report, at least some NYCH bankers understood its role as the holder of the country's banking reserve and had the power and instruments available to have prevented banking panics. How then do we explain its failure to have authorized the pooling of reserves in the post-1873 panics? Isn't there an inconsistency in maintaining that the NYCH understood how to prevent banking panics yet refused to adopt reserve pooling? Agreement had been reached to pool reserves in 1873. Why wasn't agreement possible in subsequent panics? Was that knowledge so thinly distributed among clearing house members that even a slight alteration in circumstances could reverse an earlier decision, or were considerations of individual bank self interest overriding? Now is the time to attempt to address answers to these formidable questions.

One plausible explanation is the provisional nature of the 1873 agreement to pool reserves. According to Sprague (1910, p. 120), noninterest-paying banks agreed reluctantly to go along with the equalization scheme in expectation that the NYCH would support a proposal to prohibit interest payment on interbank balances. However, when the Clearing House subsequently failed to act, the opposition to equalization firmed, and reserve pooling was never employed again during banking panics. There were apparently irreconcilable differences between interest- and noninterest-paying clearing house banks. Noninterest-paying banks regarded the source of banking panics to be the volatility of interest-paying bankers' balances. Why should they be called upon to bail out those banks whose behavior was responsible for the problem? Rent-seeking considerations reemerged as a determinant of NYCH bank behavior.

Opposition to equalization also arose because some banks in 1873 attempted, some successfully, to evade the pooling arrangement. Instead of placing newly received greenbacks in the special pool, these banks treated them as "special deposits" which were excluded from the pool. They then replaced the greenbacks with national bank notes which were paid out over the counter. Such practices weakened trust among the participating banks, thereby making continued cooperation more difficult.

Opposition to reserve pooling conceivably may have arisen from a perception that the reserve equalization scheme had failed to prevent the suspension of cash payments in 1873. But, as we have seen, the New York banks continued to pay out cash freely without constraint to interior banks, keeping bank suspensions to a minimum. In subsequent panics, the Clearing House banks conserved cash.

The failure of the NYCH to have eliminated interest payment on bankers' balances, however, did not preclude cooperation on the part of the noninterest-paying banks. Sprague thought their willingness to cooperate was contingent upon their finding another remedy, that remedy being differential reserve requirements. Interest-paying banks should be required to hold larger reserves than the noninterest-paying banks. But unlike interest payments on interbank deposits which depended on the discretion of the NYCH, reserve requirement changes called for new legislation. And there is no evidence that Congress viewed such legislation with favor.

There is a third reason which we have advanced why the NYCH agreed to equalization in 1873 and rejected it in later panics, and that is a failure of bold and effective leadership. George S. Coe provided that leadership in 1873. His knowledge and understanding of banking panics as revealed in the Coe Report was unrivaled. Of course, it is possible to argue that a purely voluntary association of banks with whatever kind of leadership could not be depended upon consistently to act in the required manner. Moreover, the administrative organization of the Clearing House did not foster the emergence of a bold and effective leadership. The everyday work of the Clearing House was highly routinized and made no inordinate demands on its officers except during a financial crisis. A permanent manager whose function it was to supervise operations did not have policy-making responsibilities.

The NYCH experience after 1873 demonstrates the difficulties in devising a voluntary scheme of collective action when it might not be in an individual bank's self-interest. Agreement was not possible among the clearing house associates: in at least two cases: reserve pooling and the cessation of interest payments on bankers' balances. In the case of reserve pooling it certainly was in the interest of the banks as a group to cooperate and to relinquish control over the allocation of their reserves. The objection to reserve pooling was not economic but primarily on equity grounds; the profligate banks benefited at the expense of the cautious and the circumspect.

The explanation of the NYCH decision to prohibit the payment of interest on bankers' balances was quite different. The evidence contained in a special report to the NYCH in July 1884, one of the signers of which was George Coe, suggests that its failure to adopt such a scheme could be attributed to voting procedure (Sprague 1910, p. 381):

This reform has been urged upon the banks from time to time for more than 25 years and it has always received the most favorable consideration. Upon two special occasions after violent financial revulsions throughout the country, like the present, it was adopted by almost unanimous agreement, and in each instance it failed in becoming a binding obligation only by dissent of two or three members whose active opposition was unfortunately permitted to defeat the wishes of the very large majority.

Although those two occasions were not specified, there can be little doubt that at least one of the two was during the 1873 panic. Though not explicitly stated, the inference is strong that the Clearing House in this instance was operating with an unanimity rule rather than a simple majority, and that if majority rule had applied, there would have been no difficulties in obtaining approval for the cessation of interest payments on bankers' balances. In the absence of pertinent evidence, it would be interesting to speculate on the origins of the unanimity rule at the NYCH. It clearly was a major obstacle to collective action even if the banks as a group suffered.

Summary

The data on the behavior of total reserves of the NYCH banks revealed that the problem during banking panics, with the possible exception of the 1873 panic, was not the amount of reserves. At all times the banks had adequate reserves to have avoided the suspension of cash payments. Difficulties arose, however, over the unequal distribution of reserves among the NYCH banks and a legal constraint on reserve availability. Reserves were unequally distributed between interest and noninterest-paying clearing house banks; cash reserves were depleted in a few large interest-paying banks in 1893 and 1907. A legal constraint was placed on reserve availability in the form of a fixed 25 percent reserve requirement against deposit liabilities. No provision had been made to suspend reserve requirements in emergencies. When the NYCH banks faced a reserve deficit, they tended to react by contracting loans and deposits; they also showed an unwillingness to resume cash payment as long as the reserve deficit persisted.

The solutions to these two difficulties resided in reserve pooling and the suspension of reserve requirements during banking panics. The reserve policy decision rested with NYCH. The decision to suspend reserve requirements necessitated new legislation to amend the National Banking Act.

The reserve power placed at the disposal of the NYCH would have been more than ample to handle any emergency during banking panics. This judgment coincides with that of Sprague. And we were both influenced in reaching this decision by the cogent analysis and policy recommendations contained in the Coe Report. That the Coe Report should be better known goes without saying. If its contents had been digested by all of the bank members of the NYCH, the history of banking panics of the national banking era would be quite different.

As we have attempted to show, even if we grant that the NYCH had the necessary power, knowledge, and instruments to prevent banking panics, something critical was missing – a catalyst that might have effectively suppressed the strong rent-seeking motivation of the Clearing House banks and declared the superior benefits of collective action. That catalyst was bold and effective leadership, which we know was present in 1873 and apparently absent thereafter. The Clearing House may not have been the most effective institution for crafting a policy of collective action. The attitudes of the interest and noninterest-paying banks to the payment of interest on bankers' balances were irreconcilable. Because the noninterest-paying banks linked the two issues of reserve pooling and cessation of interest payments, reserve pooling was dropped from the Clearing House agenda after 1873. Could strong and persuasive leadership have led to a reconciliation between the two adversaries and thereby enabled the Clearing House banks to pool reserves? If banking panics were preventable, the answer is yes. If the answer is negative, we must look elsewhere for a solution the bank panic problem of the national banking era.

7   Epilogue

For almost ninety years Sprague's classic study for the National Monetary Commission has remained the standard work on the banking disturbances of the national banking era. No other American economist had stated either more clearly or more persuasively what the responsibilities were of the NYCH banks as holders of the ultimate banking reserve for the prevention of banking panics. Sprague was simply drawing upon the inspiration he had received from having read the Coe Report, a document he rightly called one of the most important in American financial history. I know of no other that has been more neglected! He recognized immediately the significance of reserve equalization or reserve pooling as a NYCH instrument for preventing banking panics. Sprague, like Bagehot before him, was a merciless critic of the policy of suspending cash payment.

Although Sprague's contributions to our understanding what happened during pre-1914 banking panics were many, there were still some significant lacunae. He made no effort to estimate the number of bank failures, nor did he pay much attention to the location of bank runs and bank closures in the interior. A more serious shortcoming, though not due to any fault of his, was the inaccessibility of information that did not become available until many years later, including the official minutes of the NYCH and biographies and congressional testimony relating to the role of J. P. Morgan and his principal associates during the 1907 panic. Moreover, data on real GNP and unemployment did not exist in 1910; Sprague could use only proxies to describe output and employment effects. We have attempted to repair this information deficit by constructing estimates of bank suspensions and their incidence in each of the five separate banking disturbances and by providing a detailed narrative of events in the interior.

New estimates of bank closures revealed that bank suspensions were relatively few in number in both New York and the interior after adjusting for failed brokerage houses, the only exception being the panic of 1893. Bank runs and bank suspensions in the interior were far from ubiquitous; they were highly concentrated in a small number of specific geographical areas. We have found that there were no banking panics in either 1884 or 1890. Both of these episodes of banking unrest can better be described as incipient banking panics that were forestalled by the prompt response of the NYCH.

Banking panics proper occurred in 1873, 1893, and 1907, one of their defining characteristics being the suspension of cash payment. The effects of the suspension of cash payment and not bank runs and bank suspensions were how the average person experienced the banking panics in 1873 and 1907; hoarding increased; a currency premium emerged; and firms encountered difficulties in being able to meet their payroll. The 1893 panic was unique; it had its origin in the interior and not New York, and the number of bank failures rivaled that of the panics of the Great Depression. One in four of bank closures were temporary; these banks resumed normal operations within three to six months. Depositors clearly could not discriminate between solvent and insolvent banks.

We have also attempted to redefine the role of the NYCH during the national banking era by showing that it had the knowledge, power, and instruments to prevent banking panics. The power to equalize reserves was more than sufficient to have avoided banking panics. Nevertheless, except in 1873 the Clearing House declined its use. Institutional failure rather than the structural weaknesses of the national banking system accounts for the major banking disturbances of the national banking era. The NYCH was not perhaps the most effective instrument for crafting a policy of collective action.

Similarities and Differences Among Panics

The historical evidence has revealed a surprising amount of diversity among the several banking disturbances. Each of the three major banking panics differed in at least one important aspect that shaped its behavior. In 1873 as well as in 1860 and 1861 the NYCH authorized the pooling of reserves among the member banks, but that did not constrain it from suspending cash payment. Nevertheless, the NYCH banks continued to pay out cash freely to the interior banks, which would not have been possible had reserves not been equalized. The legal tender reserve of the six largest New York banks holding the bulk of bankers' balances fell to a little less than $6 million before it began to turn up. This behavior was not repeated in subsequent panics; the Clearing House refrained from reserve pooling, and the banks conserved cash rather than paying it out freely.

In 1893 the panic had its origin in the interior. The NYCH was less sensitive to what was happening in the interior than to events in the central money market; the member banks did not feel the same sense of urgency and responsibility for shoring up interior banks that they felt toward their own. A similar problem arose in 1907. The panic originated with the trust companies in New York who were not members of the NYCH. The failure of the NYCH to act promptly created a leadership vacuum, which was immediately filled by J. P. Morgan and his associates. The response in 1884 and 1890 was prompt and effective because there was no confusion about responsibility. The NYCH was prepared to help its own members.

But the diversity of the banking panics should not obscure their similarities. What the three full-scale banking panics had in common was the loss of depositor confidence resulting in the substitution of deposits for cash, which manifest itself more keenly after the suspension of cash payment. The loss of depositor confidence was not necessarily country-wide; it was confined to specific regions or smaller geographical areas without noticeable effects elsewhere. There never was a citywide loss of depositor confidence in New York City even at the peak of a banking panic. Unfortunately, the geographical incidence of the loss of depositor confidence cannot be observed because of the absence of appropriate data. For the period of the Great Depression I was able to use federal reserve notes in circulation by Federal Reserve District, but no such information exists for the national banking era.

What can be observed, however, is the loss of confidence of country banks who held bankers' balances in New York. Withdrawal of these balances reflected uncertainty about the ability of the New York banks to continue to pay out cash as well as the country banks' ability to meet unexpected customer demands. The depletion of the reserves of the New York banks was reflected immediately in the behavior of the call money and commercial paper rates and a sharp curtailment in credit availability. The role of the country banks in contributing to banking instability has not received the same attention as the loss of depositor confidence.

What does the banking panic evidence tell us about bank contagion? Was it a prominent characteristic of post-Civil War banking panics? The incidence of bank contagion obviously depends on the severity of the banking panic. Neither the 1873 nor the 1907 panics was extensive if judged solely by the number of bank suspensions or bank runs. The 1893 panic, however, was quite different. There were city-wide runs in Denver, Chicago, Omaha, Portland, and Louisville, fully chronicled in this narrative. Bank contagion characterized depositor behavior more frequently among the savings banks whose depositors were sometime of ethnic origin, especially in Chicago, and usually deposits were of small amount. Moreover, the information deficit among depositors was especially large. Usually panic spread rapidly to all corners of the city when depositor confidence in the savings banks collapsed. To allay the panic the savings banks resorted to their legal right to postpone payment for thirty days, but that did not deter depositors from returning thirty days later and withdrawing their funds. To say that bank contagion was exaggerated is to refer to a literature that has not been identified. It certainly was not exaggerated in 1893. Nor do I know who exaggerated it in 1907.

Contrast with Panics of the Great Depression

The banking panics of the Great Depression differed from those of the national banking era with respect to cyclical timing, number, and incidence of bank failures, and the structure of the banking system. They occurred in a financial environment that presumably had been transformed by the Federal Reserve. Each of the panics of the national banking era was associated with a separate cyclical downturn, but the panics of the Great Depression were multiple panics occurring within the same cyclical contraction (1929–33). There were, however, two separate bank panic episodes in June and July 1893. The ending of the pre-1914 panics resulted in a deceleration of bank closures accompanied by dishoarding and an increase in depositor confidence. That did not happen during the panics of the Great Depression. Bank failures decelerated, but there was no decline in hoarding; there was no increase in depositor confidence. Confidence in the banking system did not improve; it simply did not get worse. Each banking panic episode began with a higher level of depositor uncertainty which was compounded in each succeeding panic, thereby increasing the vulnerability of the banks to new shocks. The banks were weakened even more after each successive shock. The banking panics of the Great Depression were more severe partially because they represented repetitive shocks during the same contractionary episode.

The panics in the two eras also were different with respect to their origins and their numbers. As we have shown, the central money market was the origin of the pre-1914 banking panics with the single exception of 1893. During the Great Depression there were no serious general banking disturbance in New York City; the panics were confined to the

Table 7.1. *Number of bank failures: National banking era versus Great Depression Panics*

National banking era		Great Depression	
Panic dates	Number of failures	Panic dates	Number of failures
September 1873	101	Nov.–Dec. 1930	806
May 1884	42	April–Aug. 1931	573
November 1890	18	Sept.–Oct. 1931	827
May–August 1893	503	June–July 1932	283
Oct.–Dec. 1907	73	Feb.–March 1933	"Bank holiday"

Source: Wicker, 1996, p. 111; National Banking Era: author's estimates.

interior. There was also a striking difference in the number of bank closures. Table 7.1 shows the number of bank failures in each of the panics of the national banking era and the Great Depression. The average number of bank failures was well under 100 for the country as a whole during the national banking era, 1893 excepted. There were at least 700 bank suspensions in three of the five panics of the Great Depression.

The panics of the Great Depression, unlike the pre-1914 banking crises, had little or nothing to do with the seasonal movement of funds or the inelasticity of the note issue. The Federal Reserve had provided the mechanism for expanding the currency in response to seasonal and other demands. Cash payment was not suspended except during the banking holiday of 1933. But during both periods, the NYCH and subsequently the Federal Reserve were reluctant to act to forestall banking unrest in the interior, whereas they both were prepared to act promptly when the member banks in New York were involved.

The Origin of Banking Panics

We have postponed reference to the recent literature on the origins of banking panics until we had set out a full description of what happened during each panic episode. Now we must ask: what light, if any, does the historical evidence throw on the origins of banking panics? Calomiris and Gorton (1991) have performed a useful service in coalescing the existing bank panic literature with two allegedly rival theories of bank panic origins. The first of the two theories descends from a seminal paper by Diamond and Dybvig (1983), which Calomiris and Gorton referred to as the random withdrawal hypothesis. The second has more diverse origins, including Chari and Jagannathan (1988), Gorton and Mullineaux (1987), and Jacklin and Bhattacharya (1988), which is labeled the asymmetric information approach.

According to the random withdrawal hypothesis, the fundamental cause of banking panics is a liquidity shock induced by an exogenous money demand disturbance. The historical source of the shock was presumably the increased demands for currency by interior banks during the autumnal crop moving season. Spring planting demands were a less important disturbance to the money market. Bank failures accompanied ubiquitous runs on banks initiated by a loss of depositor confidence. Bank runs were a rational response dictated by a first come, first served rule for allocating deposits at the time of withdrawal.

The rival theory also treats banking panics as a rational depositor response to an asymmetric information deficit. Depositors do not have access to the same information as do the banks on the quality of the bank's loan portfolio, since bank loans are not tradeable assets. Asset shocks in the form, for example, of faulty investment decisions, bad macroeconomic news, malfeasance, and mismanagement are the fundamental causes of banking panics. Since depositors cannot discriminate between solvent and insolvent banks, a general run on all or a large group of banks occurs. The bank run is the mechanism for eliminating unsound banks in the absence of bank cooperation.

The random withdrawal hypothesis is fully consistent with the conventional view that the demand for cash by interior banks during the crop moving season was a necessary precondition for a banking panic, if not necessarily its cause. The NYCH banks were not always prepared to meet expected deposit withdrawals during the crop moving season; in fact, they rarely were. Any unexpected shock was sufficient to disconcert depositors and trigger runs on banks. Calomiris and Gorton (1991) categorically rejected the traditional view. They presumed to test the random withdrawal hypothesis by examining pre-panic period withdrawals to determine whether they were abnormal. They found no evidence to support the view that panics were preceded by large withdrawals. Neither have we been able to find evidence that seasonal deposit withdrawals were the main cause of the national banking era panics. Neither the 1884 nor the 1893 banking disturbances occurred during the autumnal crop moving season. And the 1893 panic was by far the most serious of the banking panics if measured by numbers of bank suspensions. An explanation that cannot account for the most serious of the national banking era panics is a very weak one indeed.

Calomiris and Gorton also rejected the random withdrawal approach on the grounds that one should expect a direct link between bank runs and bank failures. They could find no such linkage. The Comptroller of the Currency's *Reports* identify the various causes of national bank failures during each of the five periods of banking unrest. The Comptroller identified only one bank closure due to a bank run. What Calomiris and Gorton failed to note, however, was that the Comptroller's *Reports* distinguish carefully between banks that suspended temporarily, that is, closed temporarily, and those that had gone into receivership to which the data apply. We have attempted to identify those banks that suspended due to bank runs and reopened subsequently for 1893; their numbers were not few, perhaps as much as one-third.

The historical evidence is mixed at best about how well or how poorly it substantiates either the random withdrawal or asymmetric information theories of banking panics. During the 1884 banking disturbance, one in four of the bank closings can be attributed to the failure of the Metropolitan National Bank through correspondent relationships, a fact consistent with both hypotheses. But at the same time fraud and imprudent management played a key role in the demise of at least four New York banks. Embezzlement and fraudulent practices are examples of asset shocks. What the banking unrest in 1884 reveals is that both approaches can be at work simultaneously, and the search for unicausal explanations can be misdirected. The innate complexity of banking disturbances has come to light only as a result of a complete and detailed narrative of what happened, especially in the interior.

Unrest in the overseas market for American securities was a contributing factor in both the 1873 and 1890 panics. Glassner (1997, p. 133) identified the asset shock in 1873 as a crisis of confidence of European investors who sought to liquidate their holdings of American securities. Unrest in the overseas market for American securities reappeared in the middle of 1890 and was exacerbated by rumors of the impending collapse of the English merchant banking house of Baring Brothers.

Tallman and Moen (1990) attributed the trust company panic in 1907 to questionable investment decisions. For some time before the panic, trust company officials exercised their preference for high-risk real estate investments, making the trust companies especially vulnerable in the event of a loss of depositor confidence. Bank runs specific to the trust companies were particularly virulent, extending over a period of two weeks without letup; especially hard-hit were the Trust Company of American and Lincoln Trust. Nevertheless, thanks to the support provided by J. P. Morgan and his associates, the latter two remained open. Unlike the panics in 1873 and 1893, there were few city-wide bank runs in the interior in 1907; they were mainly bank-specific. Although

Calomiris and Gorton (1991) prefer the asymmetric information approach in their study of the panics of the national banking era, they did not make any effort to identify specific asset shocks associated with each banking disturbance. The task is made more difficult by the lack of available portfolio information for the troubled banks.

Banking Panics and Banking Reform

Banking panics of the national banking era have derived whatever enduring interest they might have from an alleged causal role in the establishment of the Federal Reserve System, not as a source of historical evidence to discriminate among rival theories of banking panics. One of the great half-truths repeated by historians of the Federal Reserve is that the Fed was created to prevent the recurrence of banking panics that had plagued the country since the Civil War. These banking disturbances as we have already shown were attributed to structural weaknesses of the national banking system in conjunction with seasonal flows of funds from the agricultural South and West to the eastern seaboard during the autumn. The crux of the problem supposedly resided in an inelastic stock of reserves, the remedies for which included institutional arrangements for making reserves more flexible by either a voluntary association of banks with the power to issue currency in emergencies or the establishment of a central bank quasi-governmental in organization with the same power. The remedies were only as good as the diagnosis. In this study we have proposed an alternative explanation for banking panics. The NYCH deserves a fair share of the blame for what happened in 1873, 1893, and 1907.

In 1893 and 1907 insufficient reserves were not the problem; it was the unequal distribution of those reserves among the large Clearing House banks. Reserve equalization would have forestalled the two panics. The NYCH equalized reserves in 1873 but also suspended cash payment! Up to the time of the suspension there had been no more than three bank closures in New York excluding brokerage houses; the panic had not yet spread to the interior with the exception of bank failures in Philadelphia and Washington, D.C., due to the collapse of Jay Cooke and Company. Confidence was not severely weakened until after cash payment was suspended.

The solution did not necessarily reside in changing the behavior of the NYCH. Purely rent-seeking objectives of the member banks clashed with public interest considerations; they were not incentive-compatible, and it is very doubtful whether any voluntary collective action through an association of New York banks would have been feasible.

Revisiting the banking panics of the post–Civil War era has turned out to be a promising voyage of discovery and rediscovery. We have discovered what happened in the interior and constructed a detailed quantitative narrative to reflect that knowledge, reducing considerably the size of the information deficit. And we have rediscovered the role the NYCH played and more important the role that it might have played to prevent banking panics. Sprague had been there before, but his contribution had been forgotten.

The lesson to be learned from the banking experience of the national banking era is: The NYCH bungled a once-for-all opportunity for effective voluntary collective action to forestall banking panics and thereby ward off the establishment of a government central bank. Voluntary action failed, and government intervened to fill the vacuum.

Appendix

The Bureau of Statistics of Labor in Massachusetts undertook on June 24, 1878, a thorough geographical canvass of the extent of unemployment in that state. The canvass was closed on August 13 and included virtually every city and town. Initially the inquiry was conducted by the police in the cities but was extended to include the tax assessors of towns as well. They were supposed to estimate: (1) the number of skilled workmen in mechanical and manufacturing industries out of employment on June 1, 1878, and (2) the number of unskilled laborers out of work at the same date. The estimates were to be of only able-bodied males over eighteen and only those who were actively seeking employment. Replies were received from all but fifty-one towns, and the absence of returns was interpreted to mean that there were no unemployed in those towns. Population in these fifty-one towns represented only 4.7 percent of the population of the state; they produced only 2.2 percent of all manufactured goods produced in the state and 13.7 percent of the agricultural products. The results of the canvass are shown below.

	Skilled	Unskilled	Total
19 cities	4,400	7,695	12,135
325 towns	4,120	5,557	9,677
	8,520	13,252	21,812

The total number of unemployed males was 21,812 on June 1, 1878.

To estimate the total number of males and females, the state census of 1875 revealed the population of the state was 1,651,912, of which 447,184 were males and 137,506 females. The percent of females employed was 30.7. By adding this percent of 21,812 to itself, Wright obtained an estimate of 28,508 males and females out of work on June 1, 1878.

These estimates provided a striking contrast to alleged reports of unemployment: (Wright, 1879, p. 7):

It has been reported, and the report has been industriously circulated, that there are from 200,000 to 300,000 people out of employment in this State; 40,000 in the City of Boston; 3,000,000 in the United States, etc. This last figure has been quoted in papers, works on political economy, speeches in Congress, political resolutions, etc. till it has come to be believed everywhere; and yet this is the first attempt officially, or in any other way, to ascertain the facts.

Carroll Wright, the author of the report, on the basis of relative population extended his estimates to include the whole country (p. 9). He estimated that total unemployment reached 570,000 – a far cry from the allegation of 3,000,000: "The absurdity of the 3,000,000 statement is readily seen when it is known there are but about 10,000,000 people in the country engaged in productive industries." A similar canvass of the unemployed was made in November 1878. Total unemployment including both male and females was estimated at 23,000 and for the country as a whole 460,000.

There are of course many serious faults with Wright's estimates: for example, the reliability of using police and assessors to canvass the unemployed; the extrapolation of Massachusetts estimates to the country as a whole; and the choice of the month of June, which may not have been the most appropriate month to obtain estimates of the unemployment because laborers in agricultural districts were employed. Nevertheless, there are not alternative estimates of comparable precision with which to evaluate the reliability of Wright's estimates. Crude as these estimates are, they provide a rational basis for a painstaking reconstruction of unemployment during the alleged period of gloom.

References

Newspapers and Financial Journals

Daily Constitutionalist (Augusta, Georgia)
Bradstreet's
Chicago Tribune
Commercial and Financial Chronicle
Duns' Review
Indianapolis News
Kansas City Kansas Gazette
Kansas City Star
Louisville Courier Journal
Memphis Daily Appeal
New York Times
Philadelphia Enquirer
San Francisco Chronicle
St. Louis Post Dispatch

Reports of State and Federal Banking Authorities

Annual Report of State Superintendent of Banking of the State of New York, 1908. Albany, J.B. Lyon Co.
California Board of Bank Commissioners, Report, July 1893
Comptroller of the Currency Annual Reports, 1893, 1920
Indiana Bank Superintendent's Report
Kansas Bank Commissioner, Biannual Report
Nebraska Banking Board, Annual Report 1894

Articles, Books, and Government Qublications

Allen, Frederick Lewis. 1949. *The Great Pierpont Morgan*. New York: Oxford University Press.

Anderson, Theodore A. 1954. *A Century of Banking in Wisconsin*. Madison: Madison State Historical Society.

Andrew, A. Piatt. 1908a. "Substitutes for Cash in the Panic of 1907." *Quarterly Journal of Economics* (Feb.): 290–99.

——— 1908b. "Hoarding in the Panic of 1907." *Quarterly Journal of Economics* 22 (August): 497–516.

Bagehot, Walter. 1887. *Lombard Street*. New York: Charles Scribner's Sons.

Balke, Nathan S., and Robert Gordon. 1989. "The Estimation of Prewar Gross National Product: Methodology and New Evidence." *Journal of Political Economy*, 97 (February 1989): pp. 38–92.

Bernanke, Ben S. 1983. "Nonmonetary Effects of the Financial Crises in the Propagation of the Great Depression." *American Economic Review* 73 (June): 257–76.

Burr, Anna Robeson. 1927. *The Portrait of a Banker: James Stillman*. New York: Duffield and Co.

Calomiris, Charles W. 1993. "Regulation, Industrial Structure and Instability in U.S. Banking: A Historical Perspective," in *Structural Change in Banking*, eds. Michael Klausner and Lawrence J. White. New York University Salomon Center. Business One Irwin, Homewood, Ill.

Calomiris, C.W., and G. Gorton. 1991. "The Origin of Banking Panics: Models, Facts, and Bank Regulations." In *Financial Markets and Financial Crises*, ed. R. Glenn Hubbard. Chicago: University of Chicago Press, 109–73.

Chandler, Lester V. 1958. *Benjamin Strong*. Washington, D.C.: The Brookings Institution.

Chari, V.V., and R. Jagannathan. 1988. "Banking Panics, Information and Rational Expectations Equilibria." *Journal of Finance* 43 (July): 749–60.

Cowles, Alfred, and Associates. 1938. *Common Stock Indexes 1871–1937*. Bloomington, Ind.: Principia Press.

Crum, W.L. 1923. "Cycles of Rates on Commercial Paper." *Review of Economic Statistics* 5, p. 28.

Dewald, William G. 1972. "The National Monetary Commission: A Look Back." *Journal of Money, Credit, and Banking* 4 (November): 930–56.

Dewey, Davis R. 1968. *Financial History of the United States*. New York: Augustus Kelly.

Diamond, Douglas W., and Philip H. Dybvig. 1983. "Bank Runs, Deposit Insurance and Liquidity." *Journal of Political Economy* (June): 401–19.

Dowd, Kevin. 1996. *Competition and Finance*. New York: St. Martin's Press.

Fels, Rendigs. 1959. *American Business Cycle: 1865–1897*. Chapel Hill: University of North Carolina Press.

Friedman, Milton, and Anna J. Schwartz. 1963. *A Monetary History of the United States, 1867–1960*. New York: National Bureau of Economic Research.

Glassner, David. 1997. "Crisis of 1873." In *Business Cycle and Depressions*, ed. David Glassner. New York: Garland Publishing, 132–34.

Goodhart, C.A.E. 1988. *The Evolution of Central Banks*. Cambridge, Mass.: M.I.T. Press.

Gorton, Gary. 1985. "Clearinghouses and the Origins of Central Banking in the United States." *Journal of Economic History* 45 (June): 277–84.

Gorton, Gary, and Donald J. Mullineaux. 1987. "The Joint Production of Confidence: Endogenous Regulation and Nineteenth Century Commercial-Bank Clearing Houses." *Journal of Money, Credit, and Banking* (November): 457–578.

Hoffman, Charles. 1970. *The Depression of the Nineties*. Westport, Conn.: Greenwood.

Hoyt, Edwin P. Jr. 1966. *The House of Morgan*. New York: Dodd, Mead.

Jacklin, C., and S. Bhattacharya. 1988. "Distinguishing Panics and Information Based Bank Runs: Welfare Policy Implications." *Journal of Political Economy* 96 (June): 568–92.

James, F. Cyril. 1938. *The Growth of Chicago Banks*, 2 vols. New York: Harper and Brothers.

Kane, Thomas P. 1923. *The Romance and Tragedy of Banking*, 2nd ed. New York: Bankers Publishing.

Kemmerer, E.W. 1911. *Seasonal Variations in the Relative Demand for Money* and *Capital in the United States*. National Monetary Commission, S. Doc. 588. 61st Congress, 2nd session.

Lamont, Thomas W. 1933. *Henry P. Davison*. New York: Harper and Brothers.

Larson, Henrietta M. 1968. *Jay Cooke*. Reprint New York: Greenwood Press.

Lauck, W. Jetl. 1907. *The Causes of the Panic of 1893*. New York: Houghton, Mifflin.

Maisel, Sherman J. 1982. *Macroeconomics*. New York: Norton.

Miron, Jeffrey. 1986. "Financial Panics, The Seasonality of the Nominal Interest Rate and the Founding of the Fed." *American Economic Review* 76 (March): 125–40.

Morgan, H. Wayne, ed. 1970. *The Gilded Age*. Syracuse: Syracuse University Press.

Myers, Margaret G. 1931. *The New York Money Market*, vol. 1. New York: Columbia University Press.

Myers, Margaret G. 1970. *A Financial History of the United States*. New York: Columbia University Press.

New York Clearing House Association. 1890–1907. Minutes. New York Clearing House.

New York Clearing House Bank Officers. 1864–1878. Minutes.

New York Clearing House Executive Committee. 1857–1907. Minutes. New York Clearing House.

New York Clearing House Loan Committee. 1860–1907. Minutes. New York Clearing House.

Noyes, Alexander Dana. 1898. *Forty Years of American Finance*. New York: G. P. Putnam's Sons.

Redlich, Fritz. 1968. *The Molding of American Banking and Ideas*. New York: Johnson Reprint Corporation.

Romer, Christine. 1986. "Spurious Volatility in Historical Unemployment Data." *Journal of Political Economy* 94 (February): 1–37.

Romer, Christine. 1989. "The Prewar Business Cycle Reconsidered: New Estimates of Gross National Product." *Journal of Political Economy* 97 (February): 1–37.

Satterlee, Herbert L. 1939. *J. Pierpont Morgan: An Intimate Portrait*. New York: Macmillan Co.

Schumpeter, Joseph A. 1939. *Business Cycles*, vol. 1. New York: McGraw-Hill.

Schwartz, Anna. 1981. "Understanding 1929–1933." In *The Great Depression Revisited*, ed. K. Brunner. Boston: Martinus Nyhoff, 5–48.

Sobel, Robert. 1968. *Panic on Wall Street*. New York: Macmillan.

Sprague, O.M.W. 1910. *History of Crises under the National Banking System*. Washington: Government Printing Office.

Tallman, Ellis W., and Jan R. Moen. 1990. "Lessons from the Panic of 1907." In Federal Reserve Bank of Atlanta, *Economic Review*. (May/June): 2–13.

Timberlake, Richard H., Jr. 1984. "The Central Banking Role of Clearinghouse Associations." *Journal of Money, Credit and Banking* 16 (February): 1–15.

1993. *Monetary Policy in the United States*. Chicago: University of Chicago Press.

Twain, Mark, and Charles Dudley Warner. 1873. *The Gilded Age, a Tale of Today*. Hartford: American Publishing.

U.S. House of Representatives. 1911. *Hearings Before the Committee of Investigation of the United States Steel Corporation* (Stanley Hearings). Washington, D.C.: Government Printing Office.

U.S. Senate. 1908. *Response of the Secretary of the Treasury to Senate Resolution No. 33 of December 12, 1907*. 60th Cong., 1st sess. S.Doc. 208.

White, Horace. 1876. "The Financial Crisis in America." *Fortnightly Review* 19: 810–29.

Wicker, Elmus. 1996. *The Banking Panics of the Great Depression*. Cambridge: Cambridge University Press.

Wright, Carroll. 1879. "The Unemployed in Massachusetts June and November 1878." *Tenth Annual Report of Bureau of Statistics of Labor*. Public Document No. 31 (January): 1–13.

Index